FROM COM

In the past decade, the Association of Southeast Asian Nations (ASEAN) has transformed from a periodic meeting of ministers to setting ambitious goals of becoming a Community by 2015. ASEAN is now the most important regional organisation in the history of the continent of Asia. An important tension in this transformation is the question of whether the 'ASEAN way' — defined by consultation and consensus, rather than enforceable obligations — is consistent with the establishment of a community governed by law. This book examines the growing interest in following through on international commitments, in particular monitoring implementation and compliance. Key barriers remain, in particular the lack of resources and ongoing resistance to accepting binding obligations. It remains to be seen whether these trends herald a more measured approach to decision-making in ASEAN. Written for practitioners and researchers alike, this important book provides the first systematic survey of monitoring within ASEAN.

SIMON CHESTERMAN is Dean of the National University of Singapore Faculty of Law, Editor of the *Asian Journal of International Law*, and Secretary-General of the Asian Society of International Law. His work has opened up new areas of research on conceptions of public authority, including the rules and institutions of global governance, state-building and post-conflict reconstruction, and the changing role of intelligence agencies. This is his fourteenth book.

INTEGRATION THROUGH LAW

The Role of Law and the Rule of Law in ASEAN Integration

General Editors

J. H. H. Weiler, European University Institute

Tan Hsien-Li, National University of Singapore

Michael Ewing-Chow, National University of Singapore

The Association of Southeast Asian Nations (ASEAN), comprising the ten member States of Brunei Darussalam, Cambodia, Indonesia, Lao PDR, Malaysia, Myanmar, Philippines, Singapore, Thailand and Vietnam, has undertaken intensified integration into the ASEAN Community through the Rule of Law and Institutions in its 2007 Charter. This innovative book series evaluates the community-building processes of ASEAN to date and offers a conceptual and policy toolkit for broader Asian thinking and planning of different legal and institutional models of economic and political regional integration in the region. Participating scholars have been divided up into six separate thematic strands. The books combine a mix of Asian and Western scholars.

Centre for International Law, National University of Singapore (CIL-NUS)

The Centre for International Law (CIL) was established in 2009 at the National University of Singapore's Bukit Timah Campus in response to the growing need for international law expertise and capacity building in the Asia-Pacific region. CIL is a university-wide research centre that focuses on multidisciplinary research and works with other NUS or external centres of research and academic excellence. In particular, CIL collaborates very closely with the NUS Faculty of Law.

INTEGRATION THROUGH LAW
The Role of Law and the Rule of Law in ASEAN Integration
General Editors: J. H. H. Weiler, Tan Hsien-Li and Michael Ewing-Chow

FROM COMMUNITY TO COMPLIANCE?

The Evolution of Monitoring
Obligations in ASEAN

SIMON CHESTERMAN

CAMBRIDGE
UNIVERSITY PRESS

CAMBRIDGE
UNIVERSITY PRESS

University Printing House, Cambridge CB2 8BS, United Kingdom

Cambridge University Press is part of the University of Cambridge.

It furthers the University's mission by disseminating knowledge in the pursuit of education, learning and research at the highest international levels of excellence.

www.cambridge.org
Information on this title: www.cambridge.org/9781107490512

© Centre for International Law 2015

First published 2015

A catalogue record for this publication is available from the British Library

Library of Congress Cataloguing in Publication data
Chesterman, Simon, author.
From community to compliance : the evolution of monitoring obligations in ASEAN / Simon Chesterman.
   pages   cm
Includes bibliographical references and index.
ISBN 978-1-107-49051-2
1. ASEAN.   2. Southeast Asia – Economic integration.   3. Southeast Asia – Politics and government.   4. ASEAN Economic Community.   5. Rule of law – Southeast Asia.   I. Title.
KNC742.C59 2014
346.259–dc23   2014038240

ISBN 978-1-107-49051-2 Paperback

CONTENTS

CONTENTS

FIGURES

This monograph is published within the context of a wide-ranging research project entitled, Integration Through Law: The Role of Law and the Rule of Law in ASEAN Integration (ITL), undertaken by the Centre for International Law at the National University of Singapore and directed by J. H. H. Weiler, Michael Ewing-Chow and Tan Hsien-Li.

The Preamble to the ASEAN Charter concludes with a single decision: "We, the Peoples of the Member States of the Association of Southeast Asian Nations … [h]ereby decide to establish, through this Charter, the legal and institutional framework for ASEAN." For the first time in its history of over four decades, the Legal and the Institutional were brought to the forefront of ASEAN discourse.

The gravitas of the medium, a Charter: the substantive ambition of its content, the creation of three interlocking Communities, and the turn to law and institutions as instruments for realization provide ample justification for this wide-ranging project, to which this monograph is one contribution, examining ASEAN in a comparative context.

That same substantive and, indeed, political ambition means that any single study, illuminating as it may be, will cover but a fraction of the phenomena. Our modus operandi in this project was to create teams of researchers from Asia and elsewhere who would contribute individual monographs within an overall framework which we had designed. The project framework, involving several thematic clusters within each monograph, is thus determined by the framework and the place of each monograph within it.

As regards the specific content, however, the authors were free, indeed encouraged, to define their own understanding of the problem and their own methodology and reach their own conclusions. The thematic structure of the entire project may be found at the end of this Preface.

The project as a whole, and each monograph within it, display several methodological sensibilities.

First, law, in our view, can only be understood and evaluated when situated in its political and economic context. Thus, the first studies in the overall project design are intended to provide the political, economic, cultural and historical context against which one must understand ASEAN and are written by specialists in these respective disciplines. This context, to a greater or lesser degree, also informs the sensibility of each monograph. There are no "black letter law" studies to be found in this project and, indeed, even in the most technical of areas we encouraged our authors to make their writing accessible to readers of diverse disciplines.

Comparative experience suggests that the success of achieving some of the more ambitious objectives outlined in Article 1 of the Charter will depend in no small measure on the effectiveness of legal principles, legal rules and legal institutions. This is particularly true as regards the success of establishing "an ASEAN Community comprising the ASEAN Security Community, the ASEAN Economic

Community and the ASEAN Socio-Cultural Community as provided for in the Bali Declaration of ASEAN Concord II". Article 2(2)(n) stipulates the commitment of ASEAN Member States to act in accordance with the principle of "adherence to multilateral trade rules and ASEAN's rules-based regimes for effective implementation of economic commitments and progressive reduction towards elimination of all barriers to regional economic integration." The ASEAN Member States therefore envisage that rules of law and the Rule of Law will become a major feature in the future of ASEAN.

Although, as seen, the Charter understands itself as providing an institutional and legal framework for ASEAN, the question of the "role of law and the rule of law" is not advocacy but a genuine enquiry in the various substantive areas of the project as to:

- the substantive legal principles and substantive rules of the various ASEAN communities;
- the procedural legal principles and rules governing institutional structures and decision-making processes;
- implementation, enforcement and dispute settlement.

One should not expect a mechanical application of this scheme in each study; rather, a sensibility that refuses to content itself with legal enactments as such and looks to a "living" notion of law and institutions is ubiquitous in all the studies. Likewise, the project is sensitive to "non Law." It variously attempts to locate the appropriate province of the law in this experience. That is, not only the role of law, but also the areas that are and should remain outside the reach of legal institutionalization with due sensitivity to ASEAN and Asian particularism and political and cultural identities.

The project, and the monographs of which it is made, are not normatively thick. They do not advocate. They are designed, for the most part, to offer reflection, discuss the pros and cons, and in this way enrich public awareness, deepen understanding of different options and in that respect contribute indirectly to policymaking.

This decisive development of ASEAN has been accompanied by a growing Asian interest in various legal and institutional forms of transnational economic and political cooperation, notably the various voices discussing and showing an interest in an East Asia Integration project. The number of Free Trade Agreements (FTAs) and Regional Trade Agreements (RTAs) has increased from six in 1991 to 166 in 2013, with a further 62 in various stages of negotiations.

Methodologically, the project and many of the monographs are comparative in their orientation. Comparative law is one of the few real-life laboratories that we have in which to assess and understand the operation of different legal and institutional models designed to tackle similar objectives and problems. One should not need to put one's own hand in the fire to learn that it scorches. With that in mind a couple of monographs offer both conceptual reflection and pragmatic "tool boxing" on some of the key elements featuring in all regional integration systems.

Comparative law is in part about divergence: it is a potent tool and means to understand one's own uniqueness. One understands better the uniqueness of Apples by comparing them to Oranges. You understand better the specialness of a Toyota by comparing it to a Ford.

Comparative law is also about convergence: it is a potent tool and means to understand how what are seemingly different phenomena are part of a broader trend, an insight which may enhance both self-understanding and policy potentialities.

Although many studies in the project could have almost immediate policy implications, as would the project as a whole, this is not its only or even principal purpose. There is a rich theory of federalism which covers many countries around the world. There is an equally rich theory of European integration, which has been associated with the advent Union. There is also considerable learning on Free Trade Areas and the like.

To date, the study of the legal aspects of ASEAN specifically and other forms of Asian legal integration has been derivative of, and dependent on, theoretical and conceptual insight which were developed in different contexts.

One principal objective of ITL and these monographs will be to put in place the building blocks for an authentic body of ASEAN and Asian integration theory developed in, and with sensitivity to, the particularities and peculiarities of the region and continent. A theory and conceptual framework of Asian legal integration will signal the coming of age of research of and in the region itself.

Although the monographs form part of an overarching project, we asked our authors to write each as a "standalone" – not assuming that their readers would have consulted any of the other titles. Indeed, the project is rich and few will read all monographs. We encourage readers to pick and choose from the various monographs and design their own menu. There is, on occasion, some overlap in providing, for example, background information on ASEAN in different studies. That is not only inevitable but desirable in a project of this amplitude.

The world is increasingly witnessing a phenomenon of interlocking regional organization where the experience of one feeds on the others. In some way, the intellectual, disciplinary and comparative sensibility of this project is a microcosm of the world it describes.

The range of topics covered in this series comprises:

The General Architecture and Aspirations of ASEAN

The Governance and Management of ASEAN: Instruments, Institutions, Monitoring, Compliance and Dispute Resolution

Legal Regimes in ASEAN

The ASEAN Economic Community

ASEAN and the World

The Substantive Law of ASEAN

ACKNOWLEDGEMENTS

This work is part of the *ASEAN Integration Through Law* project conducted by the National University of Singapore's Centre for International Law. The directors of the project are Professor J. H. H. Weiler, Associate Professor Michael Ewing-Chow, and Dr Tan Hsien-Li. I express my deep gratitude to them for their vision and their support.

The text was drafted with invaluable research assistance from Melvelyn S. Barrozo, Janahan Thiru and Michelle Virgiany. It benefited in the early stages from conversations with Adijaya Yusuf, and in draft from the insightful comments of Davinia Abdul Aziz, Termsak Chalermpalanupap, Michael Ewing-Chow, Laurence R. Helfer, Rodolfo Severino, Edmund Sim, Kevin Tan Y. L., Simon S. C. Tay, J. H. H. Weiler and two anonymous reviewers.

Errors and omissions remain the author's alone.

Introduction

It is sometimes seen as paradoxical that Asia – the most populous and economically dynamic region on the planet – is the most lacking in formal intergovernmental structures. There is no regional framework comparable to the African Union, the Organization of American States or the European Union; in the United Nations, the Asia-Pacific Group of fifty-three states rarely adopts common positions on issues and discusses only candidacies for international posts. Such sub-regional groupings that exist within Asia have tended to coalesce around shared national interests rather than shared identity.[1]

In part this is due to the diversity of the continent. Indeed, the very concept of 'Asia' derives from a term used in Ancient Greece rather than indigenous political or historic roots. Today, regional cohesion is complicated by the need to accommodate the great power interests of China and India.[2] But the limited nature of regional bodies is also consistent with a general wariness of delegating sovereignty to international organisations. Asian countries, for example, have by far the lowest rate of acceptance of the compulsory jurisdiction of the International Court of Justice (ICJ) and membership of the International Criminal Court (ICC); they are also least likely to have signed

---

[1] See further Kishore Mahbubani and Simon Chesterman, 'Asia's Role in Global Governance' (World Economic Forum, Singapore, January 2010).

[2] See, e.g., David Arase, 'Non-Traditional Security in China–ASEAN Cooperation: The Institutionalization of Regional Security Cooperation and the Evolution of East Asian Regionalism', *Asian Survey*, 50(4) (2010), 808.

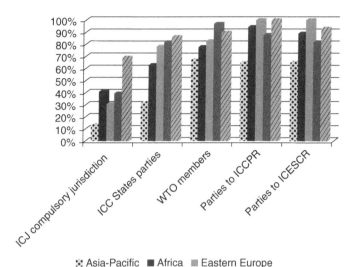

✖ Asia-Pacific ■ Africa ■ Eastern Europe
■ Latin America & Caribbean States ⁄⁄ Western Europe and Others

Figure 0.1   Percentage of states participating in certain
international institutions by UN regional groupings

conventions such as the International Covenant on Civil and
Political Rights (ICCPR) or the International Covenant on
Economic, Social and Cultural Rights (ICESCR), or to have
joined the World Trade Organization (WTO). Figure 0.1 shows
the participation of states in different international institutions.

   For most of its history, the Association of Southeast
Asian Nations (ASEAN) reflected such wariness. Its founda-
tional document, the Bangkok Declaration, essentially stated a
few shared goals and announced an annual meeting of foreign
ministers.[3]

---

[3] The ASEAN Declaration (Bangkok Declaration), Indonesia–Malaysia–
Philippines–Singapore–Thailand, done at Bangkok, 8 August 1967. See
generally Sheldon Simon, 'ASEAN and Multilateralism: The Long,

In the past decade, however, ASEAN has undergone a transformation from a periodic meeting of ministers to setting ambitious goals of becoming an 'ASEAN Community' by 2015. Building on the adoption of a Charter that entered into force in 2008, this seeks to create an Economic Community, a Political-Security Community and a Socio-Cultural Community. In contrast with weak groupings such as the Shanghai Cooperation Organisation (SCO) and the South Asian Association for Regional Cooperation (SAARC), ASEAN has positioned itself at the centre of Asian regionalism through hub and spoke arrangements with China, India, Korea and Japan, and is arguably the most important Asian international organisation in the history of the continent.

An important tension in this transformation is the question of whether the 'ASEAN Way' – defined by consultation and consensus, rather than enforceable obligations – is consistent with the establishment of a community governed by law. The National University of Singapore's *Integration Through Law* (*ITL*) project takes seriously the ASEAN claim to desire compliance with the various obligations that are the foundation of the new communities. An important part of any compliance regime is the knowledge of which steps towards compliance have in fact been taken. Such knowledge presumes the collection of data on compliance, either for self-assessment or evaluative purposes.

Bumpy Road to Community', *Contemporary Southeast Asia*, 30(2) (2008), 264.

In this book, the collection of those data will be referred to as 'monitoring'.[4] The term will be used broadly to embrace any institution, process or practice (including informal practices) that gathers or shares information about whether or to what extent an ASEAN obligation has been (a) complied with, in the sense of substantive compliance, or (b) implemented, in the sense of formal compliance. Chapter 1 surveys ASEAN's evolving approach to monitoring and the various mechanisms that have been put in place to monitor compliance in its three pillars: economic, political-security and socio-cultural. Such mechanisms are not limited to formal monitoring regimes but may also include informal and non-state mechanisms. It is important to stress that this study does not reach conclusions as to whether each of the various monitoring regimes have been effective in practice. Instead, the focus is on the institutional design of the various monitoring regimes.

As the survey reveals, gathering data on compliance is an important reason why monitoring takes place – but it is not the only reason. In the literature on the intersection between international law and international relations, important distinctions are drawn between implementation, compliance and effectiveness.[5] As Paul Szasz noted in a volume dedicated to the

[4] Cf. Winfried Lang, 'Is It Monitoring or Compliance-Control?', in Paul C. Szasz (ed.), *Administrative and Expert Monitoring of International Treaties* (Ardsley, NY: Transnational Publishers, 1999), p. 255 (defining monitoring as '[t]he actual behavior of states *vis-à-vis* their obligations . . . by means of collecting data [and] screening national reports').

[5] See Kal Raustiala and Anne-Marie Slaughter, 'International Law, International Relations and Compliance', in Walter Carlsnaes, Walter Risse and Beth A. Simmons (eds.), *Handbook of International Relations* (London: Sage, 2002).

role of monitoring, the goal is typically not punishing non-compliance but assisting states 'to improve and enhance compliance with treaty obligations'.[6] Drawing on the survey of ASEAN and other examples of monitoring, Chapter 2 develops a taxonomy of purposes to be served by monitoring. In addition to assessing substantive and formal compliance (described here as *compliance sensu stricto* and *implementation* respectively), monitoring may provide an authoritative *interpretation* of the content of an obligation or the framework for taking on future obligations. A fourth purpose of monitoring may be the *facilitation* of long-term implementation through such measures as confidence-building and technology transfers. A fifth purpose may be purely *symbolic*: certain monitoring mechanisms are best understood as an expression of unity or of seriousness about an issue, rather than an intention to be bound by and comply with the precise content of a given obligation. Having developed this taxonomy, Chapter 2 shows the way in which the willingness to accept monitoring in general has increased over time, as has the preparedness to create monitoring mechanisms for compliance and implementation, rather than simply for interpretive, facilitative or symbolic purposes. That trend is particularly clear with respect to ASEAN's nascent Economic Community, where there is growing tolerance for objective third-party monitoring which is more insulated from political pressure.

Finally, Chapter 3 offers a 'toolkit' of monitoring possibilities to guide future practice. Assuming a coherent

---

[6] Paul C. Szasz, 'Introduction', in Paul C. Szasz (ed.), *Administrative and Expert Monitoring of International Treaties*, p. 15.

answer to the question of *why* monitoring is being undertaken, this chapter outlines how mechanisms to fulfil the relevant function might be structured. Important variables include who is monitoring, how data are collected, when monitoring takes place, what powers the monitors have and the transparency of the monitoring process.

The aim here is not to offer an explanation of compliance with international obligations in ASEAN generally. The more modest goal is to answer three questions central to ASEAN's development as a rules-based legal entity: *what* forms of monitoring have been used to date; *why* these mechanisms were implemented and the extent to which they have been successful; and *how* best practices could improve on that record. As we shall see, the failure to create strong monitoring mechanisms is not accidental. In the coming years, a key challenge for ASEAN will be whether the trend from either no monitoring or purely symbolic or facilitative monitoring can be continued.

Chapter 1

ASEAN's Approach to Monitoring

Historically, ASEAN had little provision for monitoring obligations – arguably because there was little interest in compliance at all. Writing in 1998, the former Secretary-General of ASEAN stated that ASEAN 'is not and was not meant to be a supranational entity acting independently of its members. It has no regional parliament or council of ministers with law-making powers, no power of enforcement, no judicial system.'[1] This was consistent with the view that ASEAN was intended to be a kind of social rather than a legal community.[2]

Over time this changed, with the adoption of various agreements that included reporting obligations. The signing of the ASEAN Charter in 2007 signalled a paradigm shift. As Tommy Koh and others argued, the purpose of the Charter was to make ASEAN a more rules-based organisation: 'The "ASEAN Way" of relying on networking, consultation, mutual accommodation and consensus will not be done away with. It will be supplemented by a new culture of adherence to rules.'[3] This point was emphasised also in the Report of the Eminent Persons Group, which explicitly linked

[1] Rodolfo Severino, 'Asia Policy Lecture: What ASEAN Is and What It Stands For' (The Research Institute for Asia and the Pacific, University of Sydney, Australia, 22 October 1998).

[2] Paul Davidson, *ASEAN: The Evolving Legal Framework for Economic Cooperation* (Singapore: Times Academic Press, 2002), p. 29.

[3] Tommy Koh, Walter Woon and Chan Sze-Wei, 'Charter Makes ASEAN Stronger, More United and Effective', *Straits Times* (Singapore), 8 August 2007.

rule adherence to legal personality.[4] Whether the 'ASEAN Way', epitomised by *musjawarah* (consultation) and *mufukat* (consensus),[5] is compatible with a rules-based organisation will be a key challenge to the organisation in years to come.[6]

Two obstacles remain. The first is capacity, including the comparatively few resources available to ASEAN in general, and the unfunded mandates created in certain regimes in particular. Writing in 2011, Azmi Mat Akhir optimistically argued that the challenge confronting ASEAN was the need to coordinate the increasingly complex and multi-sectoral activities being undertaken in ASEAN's name.[7] The mandate

---

[4] Report of the Eminent Persons Group on the ASEAN Charter (ASEAN, Jakarta, December 2006), para. 43: 'By embarking on building the ASEAN Community, ASEAN has clearly signalled its commitment to move from an Association towards a more structured Intergovernmental Organisation, in the context of legally binding rules and agreements. In this regard, ASEAN should have legal personality.'

[5] Zakirul Hafez, *The Dimensions of Regional Trade Integration in Southeast Asia* (Ardsley, NY: Transnational Publishers, 2004), pp. 119–23.

[6] Cf. Koh Kheng-Lian and Nicholas Robinson, 'Strengthening Sustainable Development in Regional Inter-Governmental Governance: Lessons from the ASEAN Way', *Singapore Journal of International & Comparative Law*, 6 (2002), 640; Koh Kheng-Lian, 'ASEAN Environmental Protection in Natural Resources and Sustainable Development: Convergence Versus Divergence?', *Macquarie Journal of International and Comparative Environmental Law*, 4 (2007), 43 at 45; Mely Caballero-Anthony, 'The ASEAN Charter: An Opportunity Missed or One that Cannot Be Missed?', *Southeast Asian Affairs* (2008), 71; Deepak Nair, 'ASEAN's Core Norms in the Context of the Global Financial Crisis', *Asian Survey*, 51(2) (2011), 245.

[7] Azmi Mat Akhir, 'ASEAN into the Future: Towards a Better Monitoring and Evaluation of Regional Co-operation Programmes', in Lee Yoong

of the Secretariat, for example, has increased – but only slightly. In the 1976 Agreement establishing the Secretariat, the Secretary-General was given limited responsibilities to 'ascertain facts or seek clarifications for the purpose of reporting to the Standing Committee for its consideration' and 'harmonise, facilitate and monitor progress in the implementation of all approved ASEAN activities'.[8] A 1989 Protocol expanded the powers slightly, granting three new Bureau Directors what appeared to be *proprio motu* powers to 'monitor developments on ASEAN cooperation and activities within their respective purviews and keep the Secretary-General and the Deputy Secretary-General informed of the developments thereof to facilitate their respective areas of work'.[9] This was extended to the Secretary-General in 1992 in a further protocol, which stated that the Secretary-General could 'initiate, advise, co-ordinate and implement ASEAN activities', including 'monitor[ing] the implementation of the approved ASEAN 3-year Plan and submit[ting] recommendations as and when necessary to the ASEAN Standing Committee'.[10] The 2004 Vientiane Action Programme included provision for the Secretary-General to report annually on implementation progress through the

Yoong (ed.), *ASEAN Matters! Reflecting on the Association of Southeast Asian Nations* (Singapore: World Scientific, 2011).

[8] Agreement on the Establishment of the ASEAN Secretariat, done at Bali, 24 February 1976, arts. 3(2)(v), 3(2)(vii).

[9] Protocol Amending the Agreement of the Establishment of the ASEAN Secretariat, done at Bandar Seri Begawan, 4 July 1989, art. 5(2)(b).

[10] Protocol Amending the Agreement on the Establishment of the ASEAN Secretariat, done at Manila, 22 July 1992, art. 2.

ASEAN Standing Committee to the ASEAN Ministerial Meeting.[11]

In 2007, the ASEAN Charter adopted similar language but a slightly broader remit, empowering the Secretary-General to 'facilitate and monitor progress in the implementation of ASEAN agreements and decisions, and submit an annual report on the work of ASEAN to the ASEAN Summit';[12] he or she is separately empowered to 'monitor compliance' with the outcome of an ASEAN dispute settlement mechanism, submitting a report to the ASEAN Summit.[13]

The second barrier is ongoing political resistance to binding obligations in general. This is not always easy to explain, such as when ASEAN members agree to stricter obligations in their WTO or Bilateral Investment Treaty agreements than they do within the context of the putative ASEAN Economic Community.[14] This second barrier is a legacy of the view that many ASEAN agreements were never intended to be implemented. The organisation itself once estimated that only around 30 per cent of the agreements signed in its first four decades saw meaningful follow-through.[15]

---

[11] Vientiane Action Programme 2004–2010, done at Vientiane, 29 November 2004, section 5.3.

[12] Charter of the Association of Southeast Asian Nations (ASEAN Charter), done at Singapore, 20 November 2007, in force 15 December 2008, art. 11(2)(b).

[13] *Ibid.*, art. 27(1).

[14] Lay Hong Tan, 'Will ASEAN Economic Integration Progress Beyond a Free Trade Area?', *International and Comparative Law Quarterly*, 53(4) (2004), 935 at 967.

[15] Tommy Koh, 'Is ASEAN Good for the Business Community' (Singapore Chinese Chamber of Commerce & Industry, Singapore, 14 April 2008);

An example of how this may be changing can be seen in the Framework Agreement for Enhancing ASEAN Economic Cooperation, which has provided the basis for agreements on trade liberalisation, industrial cooperation and foreign direct investment.[16] The possibility of majority voting was considered in the 1996 Protocol on Dispute Settlement Mechanism for ASEAN economic agreements.[17] This was never implemented, but was superseded in 2004 by another protocol that went further in providing for a 'negative consensus' model under which the Senior Economic Officials Meeting (SEOM) would have to decide by consensus *not* to set up a panel, adopt a panel report, adopt an appeal report or authorise retaliation.[18]

How these tensions are resolved, and how the limitations of capacity and political resistance are overcome, will

Bernard K. M. Tai, 'Can We Do Anything About the Unimplemented ASEAN Agreements?', in Lee Yoong Yoong (ed.), *ASEAN Matters! Reflecting on the Association of Southeast Asian Nations.*

[16] See Paul Davidson, 'The ASEAN Way and Role of Law in ASEAN Economic Cooperation', *Singapore Year Book of International Law*, 8 (2004), 165.

[17] ASEAN Protocol on Dispute Settlement Mechanism, done at Manila, 20 November 1996, in force 26 May 1998.

[18] ASEAN Protocol on Enhanced Dispute Settlement Mechanism, done at Vientiane, 29 November 2004, in force 29 November 2004, arts. 5(1), 9(1), 12(13), 16(6), 16(8); Rodolfo Severino, *Southeast Asia in Search of an ASEAN Community: Insights from the Former ASEAN Secretary-General* (Singapore: ISEAS Publications, 2006), p. 35; Joel Vander Kooi, 'The ASEAN Enhanced Dispute Settlement Mechanism', *New York International Law Review*, 20 (2007), 1.

have a significant impact on the progress towards a meaningful Community by 2015. A starting point is gathering data on compliance and implementation. This chapter surveys the various mechanisms that have been used to monitor ASEAN obligations over time. It is divided into three sections, considering the economic, political-security and socio-cultural pillars respectively. Predictably, there has been more attention to the monitoring of economic obligations, but there have also been interesting innovations in the two other pillars.

1.1 Economic Community

As indicated earlier, the history of ASEAN agreements has not always seen a strong focus on monitoring of implementation. This section briefly summarises efforts at monitoring of implementation in the economic sphere. Key questions include the entity tasked with monitoring, the activities being monitored and to whom the information gathered is transmitted (if anyone). The first subsection examines some of the efforts to monitor specific obligations, while the second turns to tracking economic integration more generally.

1.1.1 Mechanisms to Monitor Specific Undertakings

1.1.1.1 Agreement on ASEAN Preferential Trading Arrangements (1977)

This early agreement included basic obligations to discuss and implement preferential trade arrangements. It also included a modest role for a new Committee to 'supervise' implementation of the agreement and for the ASEAN

Secretariat to 'monitor' it. Neither was given a budget or a timeline for reporting on their activities:

> The ASEAN Committee on Trade and Tourism ... is hereby directed and authorised to conduct trade negotiations within the framework of this Agreement and to review and supervise the implementation of the Agreement. In respect of all matters concerning the implementation of the Agreement, all decisions of the Committee shall be taken by consensus. The ASEAN Secretariat shall monitor the implementation of Agreement pursuant to Article III 2.8 of the Agreement on the Establishment of the ASEAN Secretariat.[19]

Such unfunded and non-specific mandates came to be typical of the monitoring responsibilities assigned by later ASEAN agreements, and of the role given to the Secretariat in particular.

1.1.1.2 Basic Agreement on ASEAN Industrial Projects (1980)

This agreement on cooperation in industrial projects provided that a Committee on Industry, Minerals and Energy (COIME) would 'review, supervise and monitor' implementation.[20]

1.1.1.3 Memorandum of Understanding Regarding the ASEAN Grain Post-Harvest Programme (1988)

The ASEAN Grain Post-Harvest Programme, previously known as the ASEAN Crops Post-Harvest Programme,

---

[19] Agreement on ASEAN Preferential Trading Arrangements, done at Manila, 24 February 1977, art. 13.

[20] Basic Agreement on ASEAN Industrial Projects, done at Kuala Lumpur, 6 March 1980, art. 13(3).

assisted in developing the region's post-harvest system by encouraging research and development activities. Funded by two donors, Canada's International Development Research Centre (IDRC) and the Canadian International Development Agency (CIDA), the programme had operated since 1977. The programme was located in Thailand, and in the 1988 extension agreement it was given an unusual authorisation to 'act as the representative of ASEAN'.[21]

It also provided that parties could request information of one another, in language that does not appear to have been repeated in an ASEAN agreement:

> Parties to this Memorandum shall ensure that this Memorandum of Understanding is carried out with diligence and efficiency and each shall furnish the other with such information as shall reasonably be requested.[22]

1.1.1.4 Framework Agreements on Enhancing ASEAN Economic Cooperation (1992)

This 1992 agreement was intended to lay the foundation for closer economic integration and movement towards an ASEAN Free Trade Area (AFTA). It assigned monitoring roles to both a new ministerial Council and the ASEAN Secretariat.

The Council was intended to 'supervise, coordinate and review the implementation of the AFTA'.[23] In addition,

---

[21] Memorandum of Understanding (MOU) between the Government of the Kingdom of Thailand, the Association of Southeast Asian Nations (ASEAN) and the Government of Canada Regarding the ASEAN Grain Post-Harvest Programme, done at Bangkok, 8 July 1988, preamble.

[22] *Ibid.*, section 7(5).

[23] Framework Agreements on Enhancing ASEAN Economic Cooperation, done at Singapore, 28 January 1992, art. 2(A)(1).

the ASEAN Secretariat was tasked with serving as 'the body responsible for monitoring the progress of any arrangements arising from this Agreement. Member States shall cooperate with the ASEAN Secretariat in the performance of its duties'.[24]

The purpose of monitoring was unclear, though it is implicit that reports would be made to the ASEAN Economic Ministers' Meeting and its subsidiary bodies, which were to review the progress of implementation and coordination of the elements contained in the Agreement.[25]

1.1.1.5 Agreement on the Common Effective Preferential Tariff (CEPT) Scheme for the ASEAN Free Trade Area (1992)

This agreement sought to encourage preferential trading arrangements among ASEAN states. It provided that the ASEAN Secretariat would monitor and report to the SEOM on the implementation of the Agreement 'pursuant to the Article III(2)(8) of the Agreement on the Establishment of the ASEAN Secretariat'.[26]

It also provided for a ministerial-level Council to supervise, coordinate and review implementation,[27] as well as calling on Member States to notify other Members and the

---

[24] *Ibid.*, art. 7.

[25] *Ibid.*, art. 8.

[26] Agreement on the Common Effective Preferential Tariff (CEPT) Scheme for the ASEAN Free Trade Area, done at Singapore, 28 January 1992, art. 7(3). On the Agreement on the Establishment of the ASEAN Secretariat, see above note 8 in this chapter.

[27] *Ibid.*, art. 7(1).

Secretariat of new bilateral agreements on tariff reductions.[28]

1.1.1.6 ASEAN Customs Code of Conduct (1995)

This document updated and revised an earlier code of conduct;[29] among other things it 'directed and authorised' the ASEAN Directors-General of Customs to 'review, supervise and monitor the implementation of the Code'. They were to meet 'whenever necessary for this purpose', with the ASEAN Secretariat providing support and assistance.[30]

1.1.1.7 ASEAN Framework Agreement on Services (1995)

This agreement sought to enhance cooperation and liberalise trade in services, building on the General Agreement on Trade in Services (GATS). It tasked the SEOM with carrying out unspecified functions to 'facilitate the operation of this Framework Agreement and further its objectives', including the 'review and supervision'. The ASEAN Secretariat was asked to support these activities:

> Article XI: Institutional Arrangements
>
> 1. The SEOM shall carry out such functions to facilitate the operation of this Framework Agreement and further its objectives, including the Organisation of the conduct of negotiations, review and supervision of the implementation of this Framework Agreement.

[28] *Ibid.*, art. 7(2).

[29] ASEAN Customs Code of Conduct, done at Jakarta, 18 March 1983.

[30] ASEAN Customs Code of Conduct, done at Tretes, Indonesia, 18 July 1995, Annex V.

2. The ASEAN Secretariat shall assist SEOM in carrying out its functions, including providing the support for supervising, coordinating and reviewing the implementation of this Framework Agreement.[31]

1.1.1.8 ASEAN Framework Agreement on Intellectual Property Cooperation (1995)

This agreement sought to encourage closer cooperation in the field of intellectual property. It proposed to establish an 'ASEAN mechanism', comprising representatives of Member States, to review cooperative activities under the Agreement. The mechanism was to meet 'on a regular basis' and submit its findings and recommendations to the SEOM. The ASEAN Secretariat was to offer support.[32] Unusually, the Agreement made explicit reference to the financing of its activities. Activities undertaken by Member States were to be self-financed, while other activities under the agreement were 'subject to the availability of funds'.[33]

1.1.1.9 Basic Agreement on the ASEAN Industrial Cooperation Scheme (1996)

This agreement sought to further enhance industrial cooperation. Among other things, it called for monitoring at the national as well as ASEAN level:

> National Authorities shall monitor the implementation of their respective AICO Arrangements. The ASEAN

---

[31] ASEAN Framework Agreement on Services, done at Bangkok, 15 December 1995, art. XI.

[32] ASEAN Framework Agreement on Intellectual Property Cooperation, done at Bangkok, 15 December 1995, art. 4.

[33] *Ibid.*, art. 7.

Secretariat shall be responsible for the overall monitoring of the AICO Scheme. For this purpose, Participating Countries shall submit regular reports on the AICO Arrangements in their respective countries to the ASEAN Secretariat.[34]

As was the case with earlier agreements, left unsaid was what would happen to the reports once submitted, and what consequences would follow the failure either to submit an adequate report or to submit anything at all.

1.1.1.10 Framework Agreement on the ASEAN Investment Area (1998)

The Framework Agreement on the ASEAN Investment Area (AIA) sought to make ASEAN a more competitive investment target, aspiring to a 'free flow of investments' by 2020.[35] It required Member States to draft action plans for implementing various programmes, which were to be submitted to a new ASEAN Investment Area Council (AIA Council) and reviewed every two years.[36] It also tasked the Council with supervising, coordinating and reviewing implementation of the Agreement. A Coordinating Committee on Investment (CCI) was also to be established to report to the AIA Council through the SEOM.[37]

---

[34] Basic Agreement on the ASEAN Industrial Cooperation Scheme, done at Singapore, 27 April 1996, art. 8(1).

[35] Framework Agreement on the ASEAN Investment Area, done at Makati, Philippines, 7 October 1998, art. 3.

[36] *Ibid.*, art. 6.

[37] *Ibid.*, art. 16.

1.1.1.11 ASEAN Framework Agreement on the Facilitation of Goods in Transit (1998)

This Framework Agreement sought to facilitate the transportation of goods in transit through ASEAN Member States. A new Transit Transport Coordinating Board was to be established, with the ASEAN Secretariat tasked with assisting it in 'monitoring and reporting of the progress of the implementation of this Agreement'.[38] The Board was to make 'periodic' reports.[39]

Similar provisions were included in the 2009 ASEAN Framework Agreement on the Facilitation of Inter-State Transport.[40]

1.1.1.12 Framework Agreement on Comprehensive Economic Co-Operation Between ASEAN and the People's Republic of China (2002)

As part of the effort to enhance economic cooperation with China, the agreement required that the ASEAN–China Trade Negotiation Committee 'report regularly' to the ASEAN Economic Ministers Meeting (AEM) and China's Ministry of Foreign Trade and Economic Co-operation (MOFTEC) on the progress and outcome of negotiations.[41]

---

[38] ASEAN Framework Agreement on the Facilitation of Goods in Transit, done at Hanoi, 16 December 1998, art. 29.

[39] *Ibid.*, art. 29(3).

[40] ASEAN Framework Agreement on the Facilitation of Inter-State Transport, done at Manila, 10 December 2009, art. 27.

[41] Framework Agreement on Comprehensive Economic Co-Operation Between ASEAN and the People's Republic of China, done at Phnom Penh, 4 November 2002, art. 12.

1.1.1.13 ASEAN Memorandum of Understanding on the Trans-ASEAN Gas (2002)

Though only a Memorandum of Understanding (MOU), this document 'on Trans-ASEAN Gas' provided for periodic reports by the ASEAN Council on Petroleum (ASCOPE) on its implementation to the ASEAN Ministers on Energy Meeting (AMEM), through the ASEAN Senior Officials Meeting on Energy (SOME).[42]

1.1.1.14 Agreement on Trade in Goods of the Framework Agreement on Comprehensive Economic Co-operation between the Association of Southeast Asian Nations and the People's Republic of China (2004)

This agreement included limited responsibilities for the ASEAN Secretariat to monitor and report on implementation of the agreement.[43] This appears to have been intended as a temporary arrangement, with AEM-Ministry of Commerce (MOFCOM) supported and assisted by the SEOM-MOFCOM, overseeing, supervising, coordinating and reviewing implementation pending the establishment of a permanent body. Nevertheless, the agreement is significant as it included a provision that 'All Parties shall cooperate with the ASEAN Secretariat in the performance of its duties.'[44] The formulation was later repeated in a subsequent agreement between ASEAN

---

[42] The ASEAN MOU on the Trans-ASEAN Gas, done at Bali, 5 July 2002, art. IV.

[43] Agreement on Trade in Goods of the Framework Agreement on Comprehensive Economic Co-operation between the Association of Southeast Asian Nations and the People's Republic of China, done at Vientiane, 29 November 2004, art. 16(2).

[44] *Ibid.*, art. 16(2).

and China,[45] but does not appear to have been used in other documents except for one adopted on the same day.[46]

1.1.1.15 ASEAN Framework Agreement for the Integration of Priority Sectors (2004)

This agreement, adopted at the tenth ASEAN Summit in Vientiane, Laos, identified priority sectors for economic integration. These were (a) agro-based products; (b) air travel; (c) 'automotives' [sic]; (d) 'e-ASEAN'; (e) electronics; (f) fisheries; (g) healthcare; (h) rubber-based products; (i) textiles and apparels [sic]; (j) tourism; and (k) wood-based products.

A general and vague obligation to monitor was given to ministers themselves, but the agreement is interesting because it echoed language from the agreement with China drafted the same day requiring Member States to cooperate with the ASEAN Secretariat:

1. The Ministers responsible for ASEAN Economic Integration, with the assistance of the Senior Economic Officials (SEOM), shall oversee, monitor and/or coordinate the implementation of this Framework Agreement.
2. The ASEAN Secretariat shall:
   (a) provide support to the Ministers and the SEOM for supervising, coordinating and reviewing the implementation of this Framework Agreement; and
   (b) monitor and regularly report to the SEOM on the progress in the implementation of this Framework Agreement.

---

[45] See section 1.1.1.22.
[46] See section 1.1.1.15.

3. Member States shall cooperate with the ASEAN Secretariat in the performance of its duties.[47]

1.1.1.16 Memorandum of Understanding Between the Association of Southeast Asian Nations and the Government of the People's Republic of China on Strengthening Sanitary and Phytosanitary Cooperation (2007)

This MOU provided for a ministerial meeting to review implementation at least every two years, hosted and chaired alternately by ASEAN and the People's Republic of China.[48]

1.1.1.17 ASEAN Mutual Recognition Arrangement on Architectural Services (2007)

Under the ASEAN Framework Agreement on Services, this agreement sought to establish a standard mutual recognition arrangement for architectural services to facilitate mobility of architects within ASEAN. Among other things, it provided that the relevant professional regulatory authority in each Member State consider applications to practise as a registered foreign architect and monitor and assess successful applicants, reporting to 'relevant local and international bodies' on implementation.[49]

---

[47] ASEAN Framework Agreement for the Integration of Priority Sectors, done at Vientiane, 29 November 2004, art. 19.

[48] MOU Between the Association of Southeast Asian Nations and the Government of the People's Republic of China on Strengthening Sanitary and Phytosanitary Cooperation, done at Singapore, 20 November 2007, art. III(2).

[49] ASEAN Mutual Recognition Arrangement on Architectural Services, done at Singapore, 19 November 2007, art. 4.1.

1.1.1.18 Memorandum of Understanding on the ASEAN Power Grid (2007)

This MOU sought to develop a framework for ASEAN members to develop a common policy on power interconnection and trade, with the ultimate goal of establishing an ASEAN Power Grid. It provides that the Heads of ASEAN Power Utilities/Authorities (HAPUA) Council are to create an ASEAN Power Grid Consultative Committee (APGCC), to be composed of representatives from Member Countries and the HAPUA Member Utilities. The APGCC is to assist the HAPUA Council in the implementation of the MOU.

The HAPUA Council was to submit 'periodic' reports on the implementation of the MOU to the AMEM, through the ASEAN SOME.[50]

1.1.1.19 ASEAN Trade in Goods Agreement (ATIGA) (2009)

This agreement was an enhancement of the AFTA regime and superseded the Common Effective Preferential Tariff (CEPT) Scheme. Five discrete monitoring regimes were established.

At the most general level, the ASEAN Secretariat was asked to 'monitor and regularly report' to the AFTA Council on progress in implementing the Agreement.[51]

Secondly, the ASEAN Consultative Committee for Standards and Quality (ACCSQ) was made responsible

---

[50] MOU on the ASEAN Power Grid, done at Singapore, 23 August 2007, art. V.

[51] ASEAN Trade in Goods Agreement (ATIGA), done at Cha-am, Thailand, 26 February 2009, art. 90(3)(b).

for 'monitoring the effective implementation of the relevant provisions of this Agreement in respect of standards, technical regulations and conformity assessment procedures'.[52]

Thirdly, Member States 'individually and collectively' are required to undertake assessments every two years on implementation of the trade facilitation measures set out in the agreement,[53] with progress to be reported to the AFTA Council.[54]

Fourthly, the SEOM, assisted by the CCA (Co-ordinating Committee for the Implementation of the ATIGA), was to 'be the main co-ordinator in monitoring the progress of the implementation of the ASEAN Work Programme on Trade Facilitation, in close co-ordination with the various ASEAN Committees in charge of the implementation of the measures under the Work Programme'.[55]

Fifthly, a Sub-Committee on Rules of Origin was created to monitor implementation of the relevant part. Interestingly, its membership was to comprise representatives of Member States but it was empowered to invite representatives of other 'relevant entities ... with necessary expertise relevant to the issues to be discussed'. This was subject to the agreement of all Member States.[56]

---

[52] *Ibid.*, art. 78(3).
[53] *Ibid.*, art. 48(1).
[54] *Ibid.*, art. 50(1).
[55] *Ibid.*, art. 50(1).
[56] *Ibid.*, art. 39.

1.1.1.20 ASEAN Comprehensive Investment Agreement (ACIA) (2009)

The ACIA, which entered into force in March 2012, succeeded the AIA and Investment Guarantee Agreement (IGA) with a single comprehensive ASEAN investment agreement. It was intended to help transform ASEAN into an investment hub able to compete effectively with other emerging economies.

It provided that the AIA Council, as established by the AEM under the AIA Agreement, would 'oversee, coordinate and review' implementation of the Agreement. It would be assisted in this by the ASEAN CCI and the ASEAN Secretariat.[57]

1.1.1.21 Agreement on Trade in Goods Under the Framework Agreement on Comprehensive Economic Cooperation between the Association of Southeast Asian Nations and the Republic of India (2009)

This agreement sought to establish an ASEAN–India Free Trade Area. Among other things, it established a 'Joint Committee' composed of representatives of the parties which was tasked with reviewing implementation and operation of the Agreement. It was to report to the parties, though within no specified time frame.[58]

---

[57] ASEAN Comprehensive Investment Agreement (ACIA), done at Cha-am, Thailand, 26 February 2009, art. 42.

[58] Agreement on Trade in Goods Under the Framework Agreement on Comprehensive Economic Cooperation between the Association of Southeast Asian Nations and the Republic of India, done at Bangkok, 13 August 2009, art. 17.

1.1.1.22 Agreement on Investment of the Framework Agreement on Comprehensive Economic Cooperation Between the People's Republic of China and the Association of Southeast Asian Nations (2009)

This agreement built on the Framework Agreement on Comprehensive Economic Co-operation[59] in the hope of progressively liberalising the investment regimes of China and ASEAN. Among other things, it provided that the ASEAN Secretariat would 'monitor and report to the SEOM-MOFCOM on the implementation of this Agreement'.[60]

As in the 2004 agreement, it provided that: 'All Parties shall cooperate with the ASEAN Secretariat in the performance of its duties.'[61]

1.1.1.23 ASEAN Multilateral Agreement on Air Services (2009); ASEAN Multilateral Agreement on the Full Liberalisation of Air Freight Services (2009); ASEAN Multilateral Agreement on the Full Liberalisation of Passenger Air Services (2010)

These three agreements aimed to progressively liberalise and integrate air services in ASEAN. A loose monitoring arrangement consistent across each was that Member States agreed that their respective aeronautical authorities would 'consult with one another from time to time' with a view to ensuring

---

[59] Framework Agreement on Comprehensive Economic Co-Operation Between ASEAN and the People's Republic of China.

[60] Agreement on Investment of the Framework Agreement on Comprehensive Economic Cooperation Between the People's Republic of China and the Association of Southeast Asian Nations, done at Bangkok, 15 August 2009, art. 22(2).

[61] *Ibid.*, art. 22(2).

implementation of and satisfactory compliance with the various agreements. This fairly loose arrangement was strengthened by a requirement that consultations begin within sixty days of a request indicating the issues to be raised. Any party could attend the consultations; all parties as well as the Secretary-General of ASEAN were to be notified of the results of the consultations.[62]

1.1.2 General Monitoring of Economic Integration

As one can see, the monitoring provisions in specific economic obligations developed over time, though there was little consistency in the identity of the monitors, scope of reporting obligations or provision for considered analysis of the data so collected. General measurement of ASEAN integration was approached with a little more strategy, though not much more in the way of structure or resources.

1.1.2.1 ASEAN Baseline Report (2005)

An early effort to lay the foundation for meaningful monitoring of progress towards an ASEAN Community was the ASEAN Baseline Report (ABR). Published in 2005, it was intended to

---

[62] ASEAN Multilateral Agreement on Air Services, done at Manila, 20 May 2009, art. 16(1); ASEAN Multilateral Agreement on the Full Liberalisation of Air Freight Services, done at Manila, 20 May 2009, art. 17(1); ASEAN Multilateral Agreement on the Full Liberalisation of Passenger Air Services, done at Bander Seri Begawan, Brunei Darussalam, 12 November 2010, art. 16(1).

provide a baseline situation that depicts where the ASEAN was in 2003 as far as the three pillars of the ASEAN Community and the [narrowing the development gap (NDG)] agenda are concerned. The baseline situation can be used as a basis or reference point against which progress in realising the long-term vision of forming an ASEAN Community could be measured, monitored, analysed and reported in the future as programmes and measures outlined in the [Vientiane Action Programme (VAP)] and succeeding medium-term action programmes are implemented.[63]

In the context of the ASEAN Economic Community, the indicators used to monitor regional integration through trade were: (a) intra-ASEAN trade as a percentage of total trade (i.e. exports plus imports); and (b) intra-ASEAN trade as a percentage of gross domestic product (GDP).[64]

1.1.2.2 ASEAN Community Progress Monitoring System (2007)

The 2007 ASEAN Community Progress Monitoring System (ACPMS) used forty-seven indicators to measure advancement towards an ASEAN Community during the period from 2003 to 2005.

The first volume summarised the progress towards the ASEAN Economic Community (AEC) and the ASEAN Socio-Cultural Community (ASCC) based on a set of pan-ASEAN indicators. These were said to include convergence of

---

[63] Asean Baseline Report: Measurements to Monitor Progress Towards the ASEAN Community (ASEAN Secretariat, Jakarta, November 2005), 2.

[64] Ibid., p. 3.

income levels, labour productivity and intra-industry trade.[65] The second volume provided country-specific indicators. Under the AEC, twenty-one indicators across four sub-pillars were measured: (i) single market and production base (fifteen indicators); (ii) competitive economic region (two indicators); (iii) equitable economic development (one indicator); and (iv) integration into the global economy (three indicators).[66]

1.1.2.3 AEC Scorecard (in collaboration with ERIA) (2010–)

The AEC Scorecard was intended to track implementation of the various measures under the AEC Blueprint and its strategic schedules. Implementation was envisaged in four phases. In Phase I (2008–9), 110 measures were identified with 73.6 per cent said to have been implemented;[67] Phase II (2010–11) saw more mixed success, with a total of 67.5 per cent of cumulative targets said to have been achieved.[68] Figure 1.1 gives a breakdown of the ASEAN Scorecard in 2012.

Such precision in numbers belied a certain vagueness in the methodology used to evaluate implementation. In addition, the expression of success in percentage terms presumably served a rhetorical benefit in reducing a complex set of

---

[65] ACPMS: Pan-ASEAN Indicators (ASEAN Secretariat, Jakarta, June 2008), 13.

[66] ACPMS: Country Indicators (ASEAN Secretariat, Jakarta, June 2008).

[67] ASEAN Economic Community Scorecard: Charting Progress Towards Regional Economic Integration (ASEAN Secretariat, Jakarta, March 2010), 13.

[68] ASEAN Economic Community Scorecard: Charting Progress Towards Regional Economic Integration (ASEAN Secretariat, Jakarta, March 2012), 16.

Implementation of ASEAN economic community scorecard under phase I and phase II

67.5% of targets achieved under phase I and phase II

Strategic		Schedule	
65.9% Single market and production base	**67.9%** Competitive economic region	**66.7%** Equitable economic development	**85.7%** Integration into the global economy
» Liberalisation and facilitation of free flow of : • goods • services • capital • investment • skilled labor » Development of 12 priority integration sectors » Strengthening food security and cooperation under agriculture sector	» Laying the foundation for : • competition policy • consumer protection • intellectual property rights » Infrastructure development » Development of energy and mineral cooperation	» Development of SMES » Implementation of initiative for ASEAN integration	» Entry into force of free trade agreements

Key to ASEAN economic community

• Political will ;
• Coordination and resource mobilisation ;
• Implementation arrangements ;
• Capacity building and institutional strengthening and ;
• Public and private sector consultations.

Human resource development   Research and development

Note : As of December 2011, the implementation rates under phase I and phase II are 86.7% and 55.8%, respectively.

Figure 1.1   ASEAN Scorecard. *Source:* ASEAN Economic Community Scorecard: Charting Progress Towards Regional Economic Integration (ASEAN Secretariat, Jakarta, March 2012), 16.

obligations to a single number, but in the absence of any weighting as to relative importance did not provide a meaningful benchmark for actual progress towards the goals for 2015.

1.1.2.4 ASEAN Integration Monitoring Office (AIMO) (2011–)

In 2011, the Macroeconomic and Finance Surveillance Office (MFSO) was rechristened the ASEAN Integration Monitoring Office (AIMO). In May of the same year, the ASEAN

Statement at the APEC Ministers Responsible for Trade Meeting noted that: 'In order to strengthen regional monitoring capacity, the ASEAN Integration Monitoring Office has been established to assist the ASEAN Secretariat and Member States in monitoring the progress of the AEC.'[69] ASEAN's Annual Report for that year stated that the AIMO would 'strengthen the capacity of the ASEAN Secretariat to track the progress of regional integration'.[70]

1.1.2.5 ASEAN+3 Macroeconomic Research Office (AMRO) (2011–)

The ASEAN+3 Macroeconomic Research Office (AMRO) was established in Singapore in April 2011 by the ASEAN+3 countries (ASEAN and China, Japan and Korea) as an independent regional surveillance unit to monitor and analyse regional economies and support Chiang Mai Initiative Multilateralization (CMIM) decision-making. A ministerial statement at the time of its founding stated that, 'as the surveillance unit of CMIM, [AMRO] plays an important role to monitor and analyze regional economies, and to contribute to early detection of risks, swift implementation of remedial actions, and effective decision-making of CMIM'.[71]

---

[69] ASEAN Statement at the APEC Ministers Responsible for Trade Meeting (Montana, 20 May 2011).

[70] ASEAN in the Global Community: Annual Report 2010–2011 (ASEAN Secretariat, Jakarta, July 2011), 29.

[71] The Joint Ministerial Statement of the 14th ASEAN+3 Finance Ministers' Meeting (Ha Noi, Viet Nam, 4 May 2011), para. 8. See generally Yum K. Kwan and Larry D. Qiu, 'The ASEAN+3 Trading Bloc', *Journal of Economic Integration*, 25(1) (2010), 1.

The CMIM is

a multilateral currency swap arrangement among ASEAN+3 members, which became effective on 24 March 2010, having developed from the CMI bilateral swap network. Its core objectives are (i) to address balance of payment and short-term liquidity difficulties in the region, and (ii) to supplement the existing international financial arrangements. The total size is US$120 billion.[72]

AMRO's website describes its functions in terms of operations during times of peace and crisis. In peacetime it prepares quarterly consolidated reports on the overall macro-economic assessment of the ASEAN+3 Region as well as on individual ASEAN+3 countries. During crises, it will provide an analysis of the economic and financial situation of the CMIM Swap Requesting Country; monitor the use and impact of the funds disbursed under the CMIM Agreement; and monitor the compliance by the CMIM Swap Requesting Country with any lending covenants to the CMIM Agreement.[73]

Optimistic assessments at its launch suggested that AMRO and CMIM might displace the International Monetary Fund (IMF) in its role in managing financial instability.[74] A more modest analysis might point to the fact that South Korea, during a 2008 speculative attack on the won,

[72] ASEAN+3 Macroeconomic Research Office (AMRO), What We Do (AMRO, Singapore, 2012).

[73] AMRO, How We Do (AMRO, Singapore, 2012).

[74] Esther Samboh, 'ASEAN's AMRO may "replace" IMF financial role', *Jakarta Post*, 8 April 2011.

turned not to the precursor Chiang Mai Initiative but to the US Federal Reserve for a currency swap.[75]

1.2 Political-Security Community

As indicated earlier, ASEAN has historically resisted binding arrangements. In the political-security sphere, it is in no meaningful sense comparable to a collective self-defence organisation such as NATO or a regional organisation with a security function such as the African Union. ASEAN has also adopted a very broad understanding of security, acknowledging that existential threats may come in non-military form. As early as 1976, ASEAN had used the term 'resilience' to denote this broader sense of security that went beyond the military.[76] Even the more elaborate cooperative security arrangements of the ASEAN Regional Forum are not intended to lay the foundations of a defence arrangement or a formal alliance.[77] On the contrary, the Treaty of Amity and Cooperation in Southeast Asia was built on a robust interpretation of non-interference in one another's domestic affairs, which included the following obligations:

Article 10

Each High Contracting Party shall not in any manner or form participate in any activity which shall constitute a

---

[75] Nair, 'ASEAN's Core Norms in the Context of the Global Financial Crisis', 235.

[76] Declaration of ASEAN Concord, done at Bali, 24 February 1976. See also Arase, 'China–ASEAN Cooperation', 812–13.

[77] Simon, 'ASEAN and Multilateralism', 286.

33

threat to the political and economic stability, sovereignty, or territorial integrity of another High Contracting Party.

Article 11

The High Contracting Parties shall endeavour to strengthen their respective national resilience in their political, economic, socio-cultural as well as security fields in conformity with their respective ideals and aspirations, free from external interference as well as internal subversive activities in order to preserve their respective national identities.[78]

Predictably, then, the monitoring obligations accepted by the ASEAN states in the political-security area have historically been weak or non-existent.

Following the adoption of the ASEAN Charter and the more ambitious goals for ASEAN, there was some movement in the political-security area – but nothing comparable to the types of monitoring that were seen in the economic sphere. The 2009 'Blueprint' for the ASEAN Political-Security Community envisaged three key characteristics:

- a rules-based community of shared values and norms;
- a cohesive, peaceful, stable and resilient region with shared responsibility for comprehensive security; and
- a dynamic and outward-looking region in an increasingly integrated and interdependent world.[79]

---

[78] Treaty of Amity and Cooperation in Southeast Asia, done at Denpasar, 24 February 1976, arts. 10–11.
[79] ASEAN Political-Security Community Blueprint (ASEAN, Jakarta, June 2009), para. 10.

Yet the action plan that followed was typically framed in the language of 'promoting' and 'encouraging' greater cooperation rather than implementing specific standards.

Unlike the economic sphere discussed earlier, which developed from incremental adoption of monitoring in specific areas to generalised evaluations, the Political-Security Community is best understood by looking at certain general standards that paved the way for more robust engagement in particular situations. The first subsection therefore examines political and security integration in general, before turning to nuclear weapons, terrorism and human rights. The last subsection considers some recent cases in which more interesting approaches to monitoring were adopted to deal with specific incidents that raised security concerns.

1.2.1 *General Monitoring of Political and Security Integration*

As indicated earlier, the basic framework of ASEAN was – and, arguably, remains – quite weak. Both in terms of obligations owed by Member States to the organisation and the resources available to it, ASEAN lacks meaningful authority independent of its members. That said, there have been significant steps over time that might lay the foundation for more significant obligations and powers.

1.2.1.1 Declaration of ASEAN Concord (1976)
Adopted at the first ASEAN Summit, this document made reference to economic and socio-cultural matters also. Yet it

was primarily significant for its aspiration that the following actions be taken:

5. Improvement of ASEAN machinery to strengthen political cooperation.
6. Study on how to develop judicial cooperation including the possibility of an ASEAN Extradition Treaty.
7. Strengthening of political solidarity by promoting the harmonisation of views, coordinating position and, where possible and desirable, taking common actions.[80]

A separate provision called for the improvement of ASEAN 'machinery', in particular a regular 'review of the ASEAN organisational structure with a view to improving its effectiveness'.[81]

1.2.1.2 Declaration of ASEAN Concord II (Bali Concord II) (2003)

Twenty-seven years after the Declaration of ASEAN Concord, this successor document sought to prepare the way for the communities later embraced in the ASEAN Charter. Among other things, it included a hortatory commitment to

nurture common values, such as habit of consultation to discuss political issues and the willingness to share information on matters of common concern, such as environmental degradation, maritime security cooperation, the enhancement of defence cooperation among ASEAN countries, develop a set of socio-political

---

[80] Declaration of ASEAN Concord, paras. A(5)–(7).
[81] *Ibid.*, para. F(2).

values and principles, and resolve to settle long-standing disputes through peaceful means.[82]

It also included provision for 'innovative ways' to enhance the creation of a security community. These included 'norms-setting, conflict prevention, approaches to conflict resolution, and post-conflict peace building' but nothing in the way of information-sharing or monitoring.[83]

1.2.1.3 ASEAN Security Community Plan of Action (2004)

Following the Bali Concord II, the ASEAN Security Community Plan of Action was intended to be 'mutually-reinforcing with bilateral cooperation between ASEAN Member Countries while recognising the sovereign rights of the Member Countries to pursue their individual foreign policies and defence arrangements'.[84] Under the heading 'Implementing Mechanism', the Plan of Action included the following provisions:

> To ensure the effective implementation of this Plan of Action, the following measures will be undertaken:
>
> 1. The [ASEAN Ministerial Meeting] shall take necessary follow-up measures to implement this Plan of Action including consultation and coordination with other relevant ASEAN ministerial bodies; to set up ad-hoc groups as appropriate; and to report annually the

---

[82] Declaration of ASEAN Concord II, done at Bali, 7 October 2003, para. 4.

[83] *Ibid.*, para. A(12).

[84] ASEAN Security Community Plan of Action, done at Vientiane, 29 November 2004, Introduction.

progress of implementation to the ASEAN Summit; as well as to introduce new measures and activities to strengthen the ASEAN Security Community as appropriate;

2. The AMM shall undertake overall review of progress of this Plan of Action. The AMM shall inscribe permanently an agenda item entitled 'Implementation of the ASC Plan of Action' in the agenda of its meetings; and

3. The Secretary-General of ASEAN shall assist the ASEAN Chair in monitoring and reviewing the progress of implementation of this Plan of Action.[85]

1.2.1.4 Cha-am Hua Hin Declaration on the Roadmap for the ASEAN Community (2009)

Adopted in the wake of the ASEAN Charter and to replace the Vientiane Action Plan, the Cha-am Hua Hin Declaration and the accompanying 'Roadmap' (consisting of the three blueprints for the discrete ASEAN communities) tasked

> the concerned ASEAN Sectoral Ministerial Bodies and the Secretary-General of ASEAN to implement this Declaration as well as monitor commitments supported by the Committee of Permanent Representatives, and report to us regularly through the respective ASEAN Community Councils on the progress of its implementation.[86]

---

[85] *Ibid.*, VI.

[86] Cha-am Hua Hin Declaration on the Roadmap for the ASEAN Community, done at Cha-am, Thailand, 1 March 2009, para. 3.

1.2.1.5 Blueprint on the ASEAN Political-Security Community (2009)

As indicated earlier,[87] the Blueprint on the ASEAN Political-Security Community did not set hard targets to be achieved, nor did it set up any formal monitoring mechanism. It did, however, include provisions requiring various bodies to report on activities.

The Blueprint encouraged, for example, the ASEAN Ministers Responsible for Information (AMRI) to develop an institutional framework to facilitate free flow of information, based on each country's national laws. They were required to establish an information baseline of these laws and 'to submit a progress report to the ASEAN Political-Security Community Council'.[88]

Though implementation was primarily left to the Member States, the ASEAN Secretary-General was to report annually on progress in implementing the Blueprint to the annual ASEAN Summit, through the APSC Council.[89]

1.2.2 Nuclear Weapons

1.2.2.1 Southeast Asia Nuclear-Weapon-Free Zone (SEANWFZ) Treaty (1995)

The 1995 Southeast Asia Nuclear-Weapon-Free Zone (SEANWFZ) Treaty built on the earlier Declaration on the Zone of Peace, Freedom and Neutrality (ZOPFAN) signed

---

[87] See above note 79.

[88] ASEAN Political-Security Community Blueprint, II.A.1.2(i).

[89] *Ibid.*, paras. 32, 35.

in 1971.[90] Each ASEAN state committed not to develop or acquire nuclear weapons, or to allow such weapons into its territory.[91] Among other things, it established a Commission with provision for decisions to be made by two-thirds majority in cases where consensus could not be reached.[92] An Executive Committee of the Commission was established to oversee, among other things, a 'control system for the purpose of verifying compliance with the obligations of the States Parties', comprising International Atomic Energy Agency (IAEA) safeguards, the report and exchange of information, a process for requesting clarification and a process for establishing a fact-finding mission.[93]

The obligations for exchange of information were, on their face, quite robust:

> Each State Party shall submit reports to the Executive Committee on any significant event within its territory and areas under its jurisdiction and control affecting the implementation of this Treaty.[94]

In addition, the provisions on clarification empowered each party to request another state party 'for clarification concerning any situation which may be considered ambiguous or which may give rise to doubts about the compliance of

[90] Declaration on the Zone of Peace, Freedom and Neutrality (ZOPFAN), done at Kuala Lumpur, 27 November 1971.
[91] Southeast Asia Nuclear-Weapon-Free Zone Treaty (Bangkok Treaty/ SEANWFZ), done at Bangkok, 15 December 1995, in force 28 March 1997, art. 3.
[92] *Ibid.*, art. 8(8).
[93] *Ibid.*, art. 10.
[94] *Ibid.*, art. 11(1).

that State Party with this Treaty'.[95] Similarly, the fact-find-ing mechanism allowed states parties to request that the Executive Committee 'send a fact-finding mission to another State Party in order to clarify and resolve a situation which may be considered ambiguous or which may give rise to doubts about compliance with the provisions of this Treaty'.[96]

The nuclear weapons regime is an outlier due to the fact that no ASEAN state possessed or sought to possess nuclear weapons, explaining their willingness to accept more intrusive monitoring. Nevertheless, it is also an example of what may be possible when Member State interests are aligned.

1.2.3 International Terrorism

The 1997 ASEAN Declaration on Transnational Crime expressed concern about transnational crime generally, including terrorism, but beyond reference to the possibility of intelligence sharing did not provide for monitoring as such.[97] Subsequent agreements also suggested the need for cooperation, but without concrete provisions for gathering or sharing information concerning compliance.[98] A slew of declarations and agreements followed the terrorist attacks in

---

[95] *Ibid.*, art. 12(1).

[96] *Ibid.*, art. 13.

[97] ASEAN Declaration on Transnational Crime, done at Manila, 20 December 1997.

[98] See, e.g., ASEAN Declaration on Joint Action to Counter Terrorism, done at Bandar Seri Begawan, Brunei Darussalam, 5 November 2001.

the US on 11 September 2001, promising non-specific co-operation with, among others, the EU[99] and India.[100]

A 2004 joint declaration with Australia was slightly more ambitious, seeking to provide a framework for future cooperation including commitments to implement the declaration – though without an obligation to report on such implementation.[101] Similar agreements were concluded with Korea,[102] New Zealand[103] and Canada.[104]

1.2.3.1 ASEAN Convention on Counter Terrorism (2007)

In 2007, the ASEAN Convention on Counter Terrorism sought to provide a regional framework for cooperation to 'counter, prevent and suppress terrorism in all its forms and manifestations and to deepen cooperation among law enforcement agencies and relevant authorities of the Parties in countering terrorism'.[105] It provided for an interesting form of monitoring through the incorporation of existing ASEAN bodies:

[99] (ASEAN–EU) Joint Declaration on Cooperation to Combat Terrorism, done at Brussels, 28 January 2003.

[100] ASEAN–India Joint Declaration for Cooperation to Combat International Terrorism, done at Bali, 8 October 2003.

[101] ASEAN–Australia Joint Declaration for Cooperation to Combat International Terrorism, done at Jakarta, 2 July 2004.

[102] ASEAN–Republic of Korea Joint Declaration for Cooperation to Combat International Terrorism, done at Vientiane, 2005.

[103] ASEAN–New Zealand Joint Declaration for Cooperation to Combat International Terrorism, done at Vientiane, 29 July 2005.

[104] ASEAN–Canada Joint Declaration for Cooperation to Combat International Terrorism, done at Kuala Lumpur, 28 July 2006.

[105] ASEAN Convention on Counter Terrorism, done at Cebu, Philippines, 13 January 2007, art. I.

The relevant ASEAN sectoral bodies involved in ASEAN cooperation on countering terrorism shall be responsible for monitoring and reviewing the implementation of this Convention.[106]

1.2.4 *Human Rights*

Human rights, situated for ASEAN purposes under the Political-Security Community, have long been controversial. The 'Asian values' debates of the 1990s were suggestive of the sensitivities, presented as an argument for cultural difference but often manifesting as a knee-jerk rejection of outside criticism.[107]

1.2.4.1 Declaration on the Elimination of Violence Against Women in the ASEAN Region (2004)

This declaration sought to implement part of the 1979 Convention on the Elimination of All Forms of Discrimination Against Women,[108] focusing on the problem of violence against women and girls. In terms of monitoring, it was an interesting example of self-monitoring. Member States committed to 'individually or collectively … monitor

---

[106] *Ibid.*, art. XVI.

[107] See generally Tan Hsien-Li, *The ASEAN Intergovernmental Commission on Human Rights* (Cambridge University Press, 2011), pp. 24–71; Thio Li-ann, 'Implementing Human Rights in ASEAN Countries: Promises to Keep and Miles to Go Before I Sleep', *Yale Human Rights & Development Law Journal*, 2 (1999), 1.

[108] Convention on the Elimination of All Forms of Discrimination against Women, 18 December 1979, UN Doc. A/34/46, in force 3 September 1981.

their progress' in implementing their commitments to eliminating violence against women.[109] They also promised to

> intensify efforts to develop and/or improve existing legislative, educational, social measures and support services aimed at the prevention of violence against women, including adoption and monitoring the implementation of laws, the dissemination of information, active involvement with community-based players, and the training of legal, judicial, enforcement officers, social workers and health personnel.[110]

Such monitoring would be purely internal, however, with no obligation to share data with other members or with ASEAN.

1.2.4.2 ASEAN Declaration on the Protection and Promotion of the Rights of Migrant Workers (2007)

As one of the areas in which the Vientiane Action Programme sought to promote human rights within ASEAN, this declaration acknowledged the importance of human rights while resisting interference in the domestic jurisdiction of Member States. The substantive provisions thus committed states to 'promoting the full potential and dignity of migrant workers in a climate of freedom, equity, and stability in accordance with the laws, regulations, and policies of respective ASEAN Member Countries'.[111] Those Member States that either

---

[109] Declaration on the Elimination of Violence Against Women in the ASEAN Region, done at Jakarta, 30 June 2004, preamble.

[110] *Ibid.*, para. 6.

[111] ASEAN Declaration on the Protection and Promotion of the Rights of Migrant Workers, done at Cebu, Philippines, 13 January 2007, art. 1.

received or sent out migrant workers also promised to 'take into account the fundamental rights and dignity of migrant workers and family members already residing with them without undermining the application by the receiving states of their laws, regulations and policies'.[112]

In respect of these severely limited obligations, relevant ASEAN bodes were asked to

> follow up on the Declaration and to develop an ASEAN instrument on the protection and promotion of the rights of migrant workers, consistent with ASEAN's vision of a caring and sharing Community, and direct the Secretary-General of ASEAN to submit annually a report on the progress of the implementation of the Declaration to the Summit through the ASEAN Ministerial Meeting.[113]

1.2.4.3 ASEAN Intergovernmental Commission on Human Rights (2009)

The ASEAN Charter, adopted in 2007, called for the creation of a human rights body with terms of reference to be agreed by the ASEAN foreign ministers.[114] The ASEAN Intergovernmental Commission on Human Rights (AICHR) was duly created in 2009.[115] Its terms of reference provided that it was to be guided by seven principles, the first three of which were variations on a theme:

[112] *Ibid.*, art. 3.
[113] *Ibid.*, art. 22.
[114] ASEAN Charter, art. 14.
[115] Declaration on the Intergovernmental Commission on Human Rights, done at Cha-am Hua Hin, Thailand, 23 October 2009.

a) respect for the independence, sovereignty, equality, territorial integrity and national identity of all ASEAN
Member States;

b) non-interference in the internal affairs of ASEAN
Member States;

c) respect for the right of every Member State to lead its
national existence free from external interference, subversion and coercion.[116]

The reporting obligations of AICHR were meagre: it was
tasked only with submitting an annual report to the ASEAN
Foreign Ministers Meeting.[117]

Interestingly, in its first five-year work plan, AICHR
sought to expand on this slightly, building on the fact that
ASEAN Member States already reported to UN human rights
bodies. Thus two items on the work plan were:

- Obtain a copy of country reports submitted by ASEAN
  Member States to the human rights bodies in the UN
  system.
- Invite ASEAN Member States to share additional and
  updated information on their country reports.[118]

With the adoption of the ASEAN Human Rights
Declaration in 2012,[119] it is possible that this area will change

---

[116] AICHR (Terms of Reference) (ASEAN, Jakarta, October 2009), para. 2.1.
Cf. Arase, 'China–ASEAN Cooperation', 831.

[117] Terms of Reference, paras. 4.13, 6.6.

[118] AICHR Five-Year Work Plan 2010–2015 (AICHR, Jakarta, 2010),
para. 4.10.

[119] ASEAN Human Rights Declaration, done at Phnom Penh, 18 November
2012.

relatively quickly. When it was adopted, ASEAN Secretary-General Surin Pitsuwan hailed it as a major development. Among other things, he said, it 'can be used to monitor the practice, the protection and the promotion of human rights'.[120]

1.2.5 Specific Monitoring Missions

A final category worthy of brief discussion in the political-security context is specific monitoring missions during discrete crises. It is telling that in each of these cases ASEAN itself was not the formal source of authority for the action. In addition, monitoring did not take place under the auspices of ASEAN except for the limited role in Myanmar's 2012 elections. Nevertheless, ASEAN did provide the context for negotiations and this suggests the possibility of a more active role in the future.

1.2.5.1 Malacca Strait Patrols (2004–)

Coordinated trilateral patrols of the Strait of Malacca commenced in 2004, due in significant part to prodding from the United States. Intended to guard against piracy, the patrols involved Malaysia, Singapore and Indonesia, and initially bore the inelegant contraction MALSINDO. The name was later changed to the Malacca Strait Patrols and the arrangement was formalised under the Malacca Strait Coordinated Patrol network agreement of April 2006. This followed the

---

[120] Quoted in Chun Han Wong, 'Asean Human-Rights Pledge Leaves Critics Cool', *Wall Street Journal*, 18 November 2012.

addition of an airborne surveillance component known as 'Eyes in the Sky'.[121]

Though none of this took place under the auspices of ASEAN, the 2007 work plan of the ADMM included support for the development and adoption of norms to promote ASEAN maritime security cooperation.[122] The ongoing patrols are therefore sometimes characterised directly or indirectly as an ASEAN operation.[123]

1.2.5.2 Aceh Monitoring Mission (AMM) (2005–6)

After nearly three decades of secessionist violence, a peace initiative in the restive Indonesian province of Aceh was made possible following the devastation of the December 2004 tsunami. The Aceh Monitoring Mission (AMM) was

---

[121] John F. Bradford, 'Shifting the Tides against Piracy in Southeast Asian Waters', *Asian Survey*, 48(3) (2008), 473 at 482–3; Tan See Seng and Alvin Chew, 'Governing Singapore's Security Sector: Problems, Prospects and Paradox', *Contemporary Southeast Asia*, 30(2) (2008), 241 at 246; Ian Storey, 'Maritime Security in Southeast Asia: Two Cheers for Regional Cooperation', *Southeast Asian Affairs* (2009), 39.

[122] ASEAN Defence Ministers' Meeting Three-Year Work Programme, done at Singapore, 14 November 2007, para. 2.1.6; Termsak Chalermpalanupap and Mayla Ibañez, 'ASEAN Measures in Combating Piracy and Other Maritime Crimes', in Robert J. Beckman and J. Ashley Roach (eds.), *Piracy and International Maritime Crimes in ASEAN: Prospects for Cooperation* (Cheltenham: Edward Elgar Publishing, 2012), p. 145.

[123] East Asian Strategic Review (National Institute for Defence Studies, Tokyo, 2007), 148. Wu Shicun and Zou Keyuan, *Maritime Security in the South China Sea: Regional Implications and International Cooperation* (Aldershot: Ashgate, 2009), pp. 96–8.

established by the European Union and five ASEAN countries (Brunei, Malaysia, Philippines, Singapore and Thailand)[124] after an MOU was concluded in August 2005 between the Indonesian government and the Free Aceh Movement (GAM).[125] Among other things, the MOU approved the creation of an AMM to 'monitor implementation of the commitments taken by the parties' in the MOU.[126] This included a mandate to:

a) monitor the demobilisation of GAM and decommissioning of its armaments,
b) monitor the relocation of non-organic military forces and non-organic police troops,
c) monitor the reintegration of active GAM members,
d) monitor the human rights situation and provide assistance in this field,
e) monitor the process of legislation change,
f) rule on disputed amnesty cases,
g) investigate and rule on complaints and alleged violations of the MOU,
h) establish and maintain liaison and good cooperation with the parties.[127]

---

[124] Norway and Switzerland also participated in the mission.
[125] MOU Between the Government of Indonesia and the Free Aceh Movement, done at Helsinki, 15 August 2005. See also Council Joint Action 2005/643/CFSP of 9 September 2005 on the European Union Monitoring Mission in Aceh (Indonesia), done at Brussels, 9 September 2005.
[126] MOU Between the Government of Indonesia and the Free Aceh Movement, para. 5.1.
[127] *Ibid.*, para. 5.2.

A Status of Mission Agreement was drafted, with monitors being given unrestricted freedom of movement in Aceh.[128]

The mission duly oversaw the demobilisation of GAM and the departure of some 31,000 non-local military and police forces. It concluded its mission in December 2006 following peaceful local elections.[129]

1.2.5.3 Thailand–Cambodia Border Dispute (2008–)

As in the case of the Malacca Strait, ASEAN's formal role in the border dispute between Thailand and Cambodia was minimal. Nevertheless ASEAN was the forum at which the issue was periodically discussed, and the success or failure of initiatives launched at those meetings affected perceptions of the effectiveness of the organisation.

The origins of the dispute lay in an earlier disagreement over the Temple of Preah Vihear. In a 1962 case fraught with inconsistent maps, a Solomonic decision of the ICJ held that the temple itself was in Cambodian territory but made no formal conclusion on the land surrounding it.[130] Half a century later, tensions escalated into a border dispute with occasional gunfire across the uncertain border.

---

[128] *Ibid.*, paras. 5.3, 5.7.
[129] See generally Edward Aspinall, 'Combatants to Contractors: The Political Economy of Peace in Aceh', *Indonesia*, 87 (2009), 1; Darini Rajasingham-Senanayake, 'Transnational Peace Building and Conflict: Lessons from Aceh, Indonesia, and Sri Lanka', *Sojourn: Journal of Social Issues in Southeast Asia*, 24(2) (2009), 211; Craig Thorburn, 'Building Blocks and Stumbling Blocks: Peacebuilding in Aceh, 2005–2009', *Indonesia*, 93 (2012), 83.
[130] *Temple of Preah Vihear (Cambodia v. Thailand)* (1962) ICJ Rep 6.

In July 2008 there was a possibility of ASEAN involvement in resolving the dispute, but when Thailand rejected the offer it was withdrawn.[131] Instead, overtures were made to the UN Security Council. Vietnam, which occupied an elected seat on the Council, persuaded other members to allow bilateral discussions to run their course.[132] Singapore was chairing ASEAN at the time and its foreign minister wrote to the foreign minister of Cambodia, copying all ASEAN members:

> ASEAN Foreign Ministers are fully mindful that how this issue is handled will greatly affect ASEAN's credibility. They also emphasised to me that if the parties are too quick to resort to the UN Security Council, this would do harm to ASEAN's standing and may actually make the resolution of the issue more difficult.[133]

In February 2011, tensions escalated once more, and again the UN Security Council was approached. On this occasion, ASEAN was represented at the Council by the foreign minister of Indonesia, which occupied the chair at that time. The Council offered support in principle for ASEAN's efforts,[134] which ultimately led to an agreement for unarmed Indonesian observers to monitor the disputed

---

[131] 'U.N. Tries to Ease Border Dispute', *New York Times*, 24 July 2008.

[132] Update Report No. 1: Thailand/Cambodia (Security Council Report, New York, 9 February 2011).

[133] Letter dated 22 July 2008 from the Permanent Representative of Thailand to the United Nations addressed to the President of the Security Council, UN Doc. S/2008/478 (2008), Annex II.

[134] Security Council Press Statement on Cambodia–Thailand Border Situation, UN Doc. SC/10174 (2011).

border territory. More than a year later, disputes with Thailand over the Indonesia Observer Team (IOT) meant that it had still not deployed and appeared unlikely to do so for the foreseeable future.[135]

1.2.5.4 ASEAN Election Observation Mission to Myanmar (2012)

As part of its halting opening up to the world, Myanmar invited ASEAN and other election monitors to observe by-elections on 1 April 2012. Invitations were issued less than two weeks earlier to observers from the ASEAN Secretariat, ASEAN Member States, the European Union, the United States, China and North Korea.[136] There was some uncertainty as to how much access the election monitors would have, but the results were welcomed by ASEAN leaders and presented as a reason for the lifting of sanctions by Western states.[137]

---

[135] Jonathan Prentice, 'Waiting for RI observers at Preah Vihear', *Jakarta Post*, 17 March 2012. Cf. *Request for Interpretation of the Judgment of 15 June 1962 in the Case Concerning the Temple of Preah Vihear (Cambodia v. Thailand) (Request for the Indication of Provisional Measures)* (18 July 2011), available at www.icj-cij.org, para. 48. See now Simon Chesterman, 'The International Court of Justice in Asia: Interpreting the *Temple of Preah Vihear Case*', *Asian Journal of International Law*, (2014), available at http://journals.cambridge.org/article_S204425131400006X.

[136] 'Myanmar Invites Americans and Europeans to Monitor Vote', *New York Times*, 22 March 2012.

[137] Li Xueying, 'West Urged to Lift Sanctions on Myanmar; ASEAN Leaders Make Call at Summit, Amid Praise for Recent By-Elections', *Straits Times* (Singapore), 4 April 2012.

1.3 Socio-Cultural Community

In international law, socio-cultural commitments are often the fuzziest, typically limited to platitudinous statements and hortatory conventions. One might expect ASEAN to reflect this fuzziness, but some of the concrete problems facing the region – most prominently the environmental issues associated with haze – have led to experimentation in monitoring linked to more concrete obligations. Such experimentation in design, however, has not led to major changes in practice, as it swiftly came up against the limiting factor of national interest.

The ASEAN Socio-Cultural Community Blueprint states that the goal of the ASCC is to make ASEAN

> people-centred and socially responsible with a view to achieving enduring solidarity and unity among the nations and peoples of ASEAN by forging a common identity and building a caring and sharing society which is inclusive and harmonious where the well-being, livelihood, and welfare of the peoples are enhanced.[138]

The document maps out broad objectives in the area of human development, social welfare, 'social justice and rights', environmental sustainability, the construction of an ASEAN identity and narrowing the development gap. (As indicated earlier, human rights within ASEAN are considered part of the Political-Security Community.[139])

---

[138] ASEAN Socio-Cultural Community Blueprint (ASEAN, Jakarta, June 2009), section II.4.

[139] See section 1.2.4.

This section will consider the general monitoring initiatives that have been established within the socio-cultural context before turning to the case of environmental issues.

1.3.1 General Monitoring of Socio-Cultural Integration

1.3.1.1 ASEAN Community Progress Monitoring System (2007)

As indicated earlier,[140] the ACPMS used forty-seven indicators to measure advancement towards an ASEAN Community during the period from 2003 to 2005. In the context of the ASCC, twenty-six indicators were used, covering poverty and income distribution (four indicators), health (five), education (five), labour market (three), environment (seven) and 'ASEAN identity' (two).[141]

1.3.1.2 ASEAN Socio-Cultural Community Blueprint (2009)

Like the Political-Security Community Blueprint, the ASEAN Socio-Cultural Community Blueprint included general commitments to certain standards, with responsibility for implementation largely left to the discretion of Member States.

Nevertheless, implementation of the Blueprint was to be 'monitored and reviewed by the ASEAN Secretariat to ensure that all the activities are responsive to the needs and priority of ASEAN'.[142] The document also provided that the ASEAN Secretariat was to 'develop and adopt indicators and

---

[140] See section 1.1.2.2.
[141] ACPMS: Country Indicators, 4.
[142] ASEAN Socio-Cultural Community Blueprint, section III.D.7.

systems to monitor and assess the progress of implementation of the various elements and actions in the Blueprint'.[143]

1.3.2 *The Environment*

1.3.2.1 Agreement on the Conservation of Nature and Natural Resources (1985)

In this agreement, which was adopted 'within the framework of their respective national laws', ASEAN members undertook to maintain essential ecological processes, preserve genetic diversity and ensure the sustainable utilisation of harvested natural resources 'with a view to attaining the goal of sustainable development'. Their commitments were to develop national conservation strategies, and to 'co-ordinate such strategies within the framework of a conservation strategy for the Region'.[144]

Consistent with these aims, the parties agreed on a self-reporting mechanism, whereby they would 'transmit to the Secretariat reports on the measures adopted in implementation of this Agreement in such form and at such intervals as the meetings of Contracting Parties may determine'.[145]

1.3.2.2 Jakarta Resolution on Sustainable Development (1987)

This short resolution endorsed the principle of sustainable development 'to guide and to serve as an integrating factor in

---

[143] *Ibid.*, section III.D.8.

[144] Agreement on the Conservation of Nature and Natural Resources, done at Kuala Lumpur, 9 July 1985, art. 1.

[145] *Ibid.*, art. 28.

their common efforts'.[146] The ministers responsible for the environment who signed the document also affirmed that the pursuit of sustainable development

> would be best served by the establishment of a regional body on the environment of sufficient stature whose task should include, but not be limited to ... (c) monitoring the quality of the environment and natural resources to enable the periodic compilation of ASEAN state of the environment reports.[147]

1.3.2.3 Haze (2003–)

The response to haze has led to significant innovation in ASEAN.

The ASEAN Specialised Meteorological Centre (ASMC) was established in 1993. Under the 1997 ASEAN Regional Haze Action Plan, it was given a mandate to monitor haze in Brunei Darussalam, Indonesia, Malaysia and Singapore; from 2003, its remit was extended to include all of ASEAN. ASMC was intended to 'serve as a regional information centre for compiling, analysing and disseminating information derived from satellite imagery and meteorological data necessary to detect and monitor land and forest fires and the occurrence of smoke haze'.[148]

The 2002 ASEAN Agreement on Transboundary Haze Pollution was a legally binding agreement that extended

---

[146] Jakarta Resolution on Sustainable Development, done at Jakarta, 30 October 1987, para. I.

[147] *Ibid.*, para. IV.

[148] Regional Haze Action Plan, done at Singapore, 23 December 1997, para. 8.

and deepened these obligations. Indeed, its purpose was stated as being to 'prevent and monitor transboundary haze'.[149] Each party was required to 'take appropriate measures to monitor': (a) all fire-prone areas, (b) all land and/or forest fires, (c) the environmental conditions conducive to such land and/or forest fires, and (d) haze pollution arising from such land and/or forest fires.[150] They were also required to ensure that these national monitoring centres, at 'agreed regular intervals', send data to a new ASEAN Co-ordinating Centre for Transboundary Haze Pollution Control.[151] Interestingly, and unusually for ASEAN, the 2002 agreement only required six parties to ratify it for it to come into force.[152]

The haze that blanketed Singapore and Malaysia in June 2013 was the worst since 1997; the severity of the problem encouraged a creative response. In October 2013, an agreement was reached to create a new ASEAN Sub-Regional Haze Monitoring System (HMS), which will share detailed information such as satellite maps in order to pinpoint fires and identify those responsible. Indonesia also expressed its intention to ratify the 2002 convention, with the Chairman's Statement providing that the group looked forward to such ratification 'at the earliest time'.[153] Indonesia ultimately

---

[149] ASEAN Agreement on Transboundary Haze Pollution, done at Kuala Lumpur, 10 June 2002, in force 11 November 2003, art. 2.

[150] *Ibid.*, art. 7.

[151] *Ibid.*, art. 8.

[152] *Ibid.*, art. 29(1).

[153] Chairman's Statement of the 23rd ASEAN Summit (Bandar Seri Begawan: ASEAN, 9 October 2013), para. 42. See also 'Indonesia's Parliament Set to Ratify Asean Pact on Transboundary Haze', *Straits Times*, 3 March 2014.

ratified the 2002 ASEAN Agreement on Transboundary Haze Pollution on 16 September 2014.

1.3.2.4 ASEAN Agreement on Disaster Management and Emergency Response (2005)

This agreement sought to develop a regional response action plan to deal with disasters, defined for this purpose as 'a serious disruption of the functioning of a community or a society causing widespread human, material, economic or environmental losses'.[154] Among other obligations, the parties agreed to 'transmit to the Secretariat reports on the measures taken for the implementation of this Agreement in such form and at such intervals as determined by the Conference of the Parties'.[155]

---

[154] ASEAN Agreement on Disaster Management and Emergency Response, done at Vientiane, 26 July 2005, art. 1(3).

[155] *Ibid.*, art. 29.

Chapter 2

The Purposes of Monitoring

As the survey of ASEAN practice demonstrates, monitoring has been undertaken in a variety of forms and, implicitly, for a variety of purposes. This chapter seeks to elucidate those purposes and offer a tentative evaluation of the suitability of the monitoring mechanisms that have been established. Chapter 3 will then offer a more general survey of structures and processes available.

As indicated in the Introduction, monitoring is often understood as the gathering of information on compliance with or implementation of certain obligations. The survey of ASEAN practice is consistent with this, for example AMRO's role in ensuring compliance with the CMIM agreement,[1] or the AMM's role in monitoring implementation of the peace agreement in Aceh.[2] But limiting analysis to these categories would not encompass the various occasions in which nominal monitoring takes place without meaningful efforts to link the mechanism in question to substantive or formal compliance.

As outlined in the Introduction,[3] this chapter distinguishes between five discrete purposes for which monitoring appears to have been undertaken in the ASEAN context. The first two are the familiar categories of *compliance sensu stricto*, in the sense of substantive compliance with an obligation, and *implementation*, in the sense of formal compliance

---

[1] See text accompanying notes 5–6 in the Introduction.
[2] See section 1.2.5.1.
[3] See text accompanying note 7 in the Introduction.

with an obligation. In addition, however, the ASEAN experience suggests three additional categories of analysis: *interpretation*, meaning that monitoring clarifies or provides an authoritative interpretation of an obligation; *facilitation*, denoting the purpose as being supportive of parties' efforts to comply with an obligation; and *symbolism*, a final category in which there is no clear purpose for an intentionally weak mechanism beyond suggesting that an obligation is important enough for compliance to be desirable.

2.1 Compliance *Sensu Stricto*

Mechanisms to evaluate substantive compliance may be formal or informal: the defining characteristic is that monitoring is explicitly linked to the evaluation of success in achieving a specified outcome. This presumes, among other things, that the outcome is in fact specified. As we have seen, many ASEAN agreements are intentionally vague in their objectives, often framed in the language of promotion and cooperation rather than the achievement of clear goals.

An obvious exception to this is the effort to make ASEAN a nuclear-free zone,[4] though this may be treated as something of an outlier given the general taboo over nuclear weapons and the relative narrowness of the obligations. Importantly, this was also a negative obligation rather than a positive one: none of the ASEAN states at the time that the SEANWFZ treaty was concluded had a nuclear weapons programme, and the primary commitment was that they

---

[4] See section 1.2.2.1.

would not begin one. A more general category of obligations that includes monitoring mechanisms intended to achieve substantive compliance can be seen in efforts to establish the ASEAN Economic Community. This is clearly interest-driven, as the goal of economic integration is measurable in a way that, say, cooperation on human rights is not.

Beyond the clarity of objectives, in structural terms a compliance mechanism may differ little from a monitoring mechanism that does not seek to achieve compliance. The key distinction may need to be found in the attitude towards and perception of the mechanism by members: tribunals and courts secure compliance in so far as members respect their decisions to be binding; a peer review mechanism exerts peer pressure in so far as members respect one another's views and provide frank opinions and critique.[5]

Structural possibilities are considered further in Chapter 3, but certain aspects may suggest a desire to achieve compliance. The creation of an independent body em-powered to investigate or evaluate and, if necessary, enforce compliance, would be an example of this. Investigations by third parties of compliance are almost non-existent within ASEAN, however, even though Member States may have submitted to external regimes such as the Universal Periodic Review of human rights obligations under the UN Human Rights Council. Evaluation may also take the form of an

---

[5] Supporting and Enhancing Regional Surveillance for ASEAN+3 and the Chiang Mai Initiative Multilateralization (Asian Development Bank (ADB), Manila, May 2011), paras. 10–13; Chang Li Lin and Ramkishen S. Rajan, 'The Economics and Politics of Monetary Regionalism in Asia', *ASEAN Economic Bulletin*, 18(1) (2001), 103 at 112–13.

adjudicative process, such as before a court, tribunal or commission, with powers to make binding determinations. Again, such obligations are very limited within ASEAN though they are part of Member State commitments to the WTO.

Peer pressure should not be discounted as a means of encouraging or compelling substantive compliance.[6] Not all peer review mechanisms seek to exert peer pressure, however. Peer reviews may sometimes merely facilitate sharing of information or building confidence. In addition to the respect members hold for one another's views, a key factor may also be the public nature of the review: in so far as data on compliance are shared publicly, this is more likely to have an influence on Member State behaviour. Similarly, even self-regulation not connected to a formal structure for compliance evaluation may have an impact on behaviour if the results are publicised and incentive structures encourage compliance.

In assessing the success of a monitoring mechanism focused on compliance *sensu stricto*, three questions are therefore relevant. First, was the mechanism *intended* to evaluate compliance? Secondly, was it adequately *designed* to evaluate compliance? And thirdly, was there *political will* on the part of the states parties such that it could carry out this function?

SEANWFZ may be an example of a successful monitoring mechanism, though as indicated earlier its scope was

---

[6] Fabrizio Pagani, *Peer Review: A Tool for Co-operation and Change – An Analysis of an OECD Working Method* (Paris: OECD, SG/LEG(2002)1, 11 September 2002).

extremely narrow.[7] The largest group of agreements with such monitoring is in the economic field, with an apparently higher tolerance of potentially intrusive monitoring. This would include the 2009 ATIGA[8] and the 2009 ACIA.[9]

Agreements with concrete monitoring of compliance would also include some of the specific monitoring missions in the political-security field such as the 2004 Malacca Strait Patrols[10] and the 2005–6 AMM[11] – though it is important to recall that these were effectively conducted outside ASEAN auspices.

AMRO, described earlier, is an interesting example of a monitoring mechanism with more than one purpose.[12] Its general economic surveillance and early warning function may be considered facilitative in nature, but a separate mechanism is empowered to assess the merits of particular requests for financial support. Such monitoring is necessary to balance the need to ensure financial stability against the dangers of uncontrolled lending.[13]

AMRO's role in the CMIM is to issue an independent report on a state that seeks to draw from the CMIM reserve pool. The Executive Level Decision Making Body (ELDMB) is then to approve the loan following a two-thirds majority based on a weighted voting scheme. Any lending conditions or

---

[7] See section 1.2.2.1.

[8] See section 1.1.1.19.

[9] See section 1.1.1.20.

[10] See section 1.2.5.1.

[11] See section 1.2.5.2.

[12] See section 1.1.2.5.

[13] William Grimes, 'The Asian Monetary Fund Reborn? Implications of Chang Mai Initiative Multilateralization', *Asia Policy*, 11 (2011), 79.

covenants would also originate from the ELDMB. AMRO will then monitor compliance with any lending covenants.[14] The main body tasked with enforcement is the ELDMB. This is significant because it departs from the traditional ASEAN consensus-based approach and adopts a weighted voting procedure in which countries get votes in proportion to their financial contributions. In reality, decision-making is likely to be closer to the consensus model used more generally in ASEAN. But the potential of this mechanism may have a disciplining effect that would encourage countries to regulate themselves.

In theory, then, monitoring under AMRO has a potential 'hard' compliance function. It remains unclear, however, when or if this will be invoked in practice. As indicated earlier, states have found other means of dealing with financial instability. More generally, much of the role that might have been undertaken by AMRO has in fact been outsourced to the IMF. This includes instituting lending covenants and securing compliance. What has been termed 'the IMF Link' requires states to initiate negotiations with IMF for a standby agreement before 80 per cent of their borrowing limit can be accessed. This suggests that the ASEAN+3 states may be unwilling to undertake a significant enforcement role.[15]

[14] See www.amro-asia.org/about-amro/overview/how-we-do/; www.amro-asia.org/wp-content/uploads/2011/12/Key-Points-of-CMIM.pdf.
[15] Grimes, 'The Asian Monetary Fund Reborn? Implications of Chang Mai Initiative Multilateralization', 96–8; Hal Hill and Jayant Menon, 'Financial Safety Nets in Asia: Genesis, Evolution, Adequacy, and Way Forward' (Arndt-Corden Department of Economics Crawford School of Public Policy, ANU College of Asia and the Pacific, Working Paper No. 2012/17, Canberra, September 2012).

2.2 Implementation

Formal compliance is most easily shown when an obligation requires certain objective procedural steps to be taken – for example, the creation of a governmental agency or adoption of legislation. The formality of compliance, referred to here as implementation, lies in the focus on the agency or the legislation rather than the effectiveness of the measure taken in achieving the stated purpose.

This is in many ways far simpler than evaluating compliance *sensu stricto*, as the formal steps to implement a set of obligations may be much clearer. In the ASEAN context, for example, various agreements require the parties to report to a ministerial body, often through the ASEAN Secretariat, on actions taken to implement the obligations. Frequently, however, there is no indication of what consequences, if any, would follow a report of less than complete implementation – or failure to report back at all.

Examples of monitoring of implementation might include the reporting required by the 1992 CEPT Scheme,[16] the 2002 MOU on Trans-ASEAN Gas,[17] the 2004 Agreement on Trade in Goods between ASEAN and China,[18] the 2007 MOU on the ASEAN Power Grid,[19] the 2009 Agreement on Investment between ASEAN and China,[20] the 2004 ASEAN

---

[16] See section 1.1.1.5.
[17] See section 1.1.1.13.
[18] See section 1.1.1.14.
[19] See section 1.1.1.18.
[20] See section 1.1.1.22.

Security Community Plan of Action,[21] the 2009 Declaration on the Roadmap for the ASEAN Community,[22] and the 2007 ASEAN Convention on Counter Terrorism.[23]

As indicated earlier, the transboundary nature of haze demanded concerted action and monitoring to ensure that agreements are being upheld. The real damage caused by haze thus required more than a 'political' statement in addressing the issue. The mechanisms first established in 1995 were unusual in that they provided explicitly for monitoring arrangements. Yet they were typical in that they did not depart from ASEAN's norms of 'informality, non-interference and consensus'. As a result, the regime had limited impact on national actions and the impact of haze in 1997 was in fact far worse than previous years.[24]

The 2002 ASEAN Agreement on Transboundary Haze Pollution was intended to be more impactful. A legally binding agreement, it departed still further from ASEAN practice by providing that it would enter into force upon ratification by only six of the ASEAN states.[25] The Agreement required parties to take immediate steps to control fires and haze, and adopt legislation to implement this. Yet the obligations were ultimately vague, limited to 'appropriate'

---

[21] See section 1.2.1.3.

[22] See section 1.2.1.4.

[23] See section 1.2.3.1.

[24] Vinod K. Aggarwal and Jonathan T. Chow, 'The Perils of Consensus: How ASEAN's Meta-Regime Undermines Economic and Environmental Cooperation', *Review of International Political Economy*, 17(2) (2010), 262 at 278.

[25] ASEAN Agreement on Transboundary Haze Pollution, art. 29(1).

policies; and in any case there was no sanction for non-compliance. Even with such limited teeth, it is telling that Indonesia – widely regarded as the main source of haze pollution – took so long to ratify the 2002 Agreement.[26]

2.3 Interpretation

Monitoring mechanisms aimed at substantive compliance may include adjudicatory bodies with enforcement powers. But an adjudicatory body may also provide an authoritative interpretation of the content of the obligation. The distinction lies between authoritatively adjudicating a dispute and authoritatively providing an interpretation of terms without pronouncing on the dispute at hand. The clearest example of this is the advisory jurisdiction of judicial bodies such as the ICJ and the International Tribunal for the Law of the Sea (ITLOS).

A related task may be the provision of a forum for negotiation and elaboration of more substantive obligations at a later date. (This is distinct from facilitating compliance and the purely symbolic processes discussed in the following sections.) The different ASEAN framework agreements may be better understood in this way.[27]

For example, the 1992 Framework Agreement on Enhancing ASEAN Economic Cooperation was unclear as

---

[26] See section 1.3.2.3. See generally Aggarwal and Chow, 'The Perils of Consensus: How ASEAN's Meta-Regime Undermines Economic and Environmental Cooperation', 281; Alan Khee-Jin Tan, 'The ASEAN Agreement on Transboundary Haze Pollution: Prospects for Compliance and Effectiveness in Post-Suharto Indonesia', *New York University Environmental Law Journal*, 13(3) (2005), 647.

[27] See sections 1.1.1.7, 1.1.1.8, 1.1.1.10, 1.1.1.11, 1.1.1.12, 1.1.1.15.

to the purpose of its relatively weak monitoring mechanism.[28] Close examination suggests that it was not intended to serve a compliance or implementation function, but primarily an interpretive one.[29] Neither the AFTA Council nor the ASEAN Secretariat was empowered to secure compliance. The formal powers were broad and vague, but it was also clear at the time that the obligations – such as they were – remained understood in the traditional 'ASEAN Way' of consensus-based approaches to problems of common concern.[30] Thus when Thailand warned that it might have to backtrack on its tariff reduction commitments, the second AFTA Council meeting was indefinitely postponed. Private exchanges between the various ministers led to a compromise deal negotiated outside the strict terms of the agreement, allowing AFTA to be implemented.[31]

A second instance was a dispute between Singapore and Malaysia over measures adopted by the latter with regards to petroleum imports.[32] Rather than bringing the matter before the AFTA Council, Singapore chose to resolve it through the WTO. The choice was natural given that the AFTA Council lacked the power to get Malaysia to comply

[28] See section 1.1.1.4.
[29] AFTA 'was as much a political gesture as an economic instrument whose ramifications had been thoroughly explored prior to signature': John Ravenhill, 'Economic Cooperation in Southeast Asia: Changing Incentives', *Asian Survey*, 35(9) (1995), 850 at 859.
[30] *Ibid.*, pp. 859–60.
[31] Ranjit Gil, *ASEAN Towards the 21st Century: A Thirty-Year Review of the Association of Southeast Asian Nations* (London: ASEAN Academic Press, 1997), pp. 147–58.
[32] Ravenhill, 'Economic Cooperation', 861.

because it required a consensus. This would have required Malaysia to vote against itself. Michael Ewing-Chow and Edrick Gao, in their analysis based on game theory, cite the lack of neutrality of the AFTA Council as hindering its ability to fulfil a compliance function.[33]

Nevertheless, despite the lack of a strong compliance mechanism, AFTA was successfully implemented. This suggests that the lack of such a mechanism may not frustrate the underlying substantive obligation. Given the many international law agreements that see compliance without monitoring or enforcement, that much is not surprising. But is it accurate to say that the monitoring mechanisms did in fact encourage compliance? Beyond general statements in the Framework Agreement suggesting that they would 'review' and 'monitor' implementation,[34] there were no clear statements concerning the roles to be played by the AFTA Council or ASEAN Secretariat. Both roles evolved over time.

The AFTA Council, for example, provided an active forum for discussion and review of the integration process and remaining barriers to trade. The annual meetings between ministers also served to strengthen relations between Member States. As for the ASEAN Secretariat, it has often been said that the Secretariat lacks the resources to conduct

---

[33] Michael Ewing-Chow and Edrick Gao, 'The Asian Economic Community: ASEAN – A Building or Stumbling Block for China and India Economic Cooperation?', in Muthucumaraswamy Sornarajah and Wang Jiangyu (eds.), *China, India and the International Economic Order* (Cambridge University Press, 2010), pp. 407–8.

[34] Framework Agreements on Enhancing ASEAN Economic Cooperation, arts. 7–8.

meaningful monitoring.[35] The gap is in the form of both data and analysis. Analysis can be supplemented by the private sector and civil society, including academia. Larger problems lie in the paucity of reliable data. ASEAN typically relies upon Member States for the collection of data, but those members may lack the capacity to gather such data or be unwilling to share them.[36]

One role played by the ASEAN Secretariat was in setting up the ASEAN Business Forum (ABF) – something not originally contemplated in the Framework Agreement. This provided a forum for corporate leaders to meet and discuss business initiatives. Launched prior to AFTA, in 1991, the apparent intention was to encourage agreement on AFTA. It is unclear how important the ABF was in doing so, but this is an interesting early example of the ASEAN Secretariat playing such a role. Much of the opposition to AFTA came from businesses which saw themselves as losing out because of AFTA. It seems that the ABF was hoped to be a forum through which domestic opposition could be addressed. In doing so, it implicitly embraced the 'ASEAN Way' of consultation and consensus, while quietly promoting regional investments.[37]

---

[35] Ewing-Chow and Gao, 'The Asian Economic Community: ASEAN – A Building or Stumbling Block for China and India Economic Cooperation?', p. 400; Ravenhill, 'Economic Cooperation', 861; Shaun Narine, *Explaining ASEAN: Regionalism in Southeast Asia* (Boulder, CO: Lynne Rienner, 2002), p. 162.

[36] George Manzano, 'Is there Any Value-Added in the ASEAN Surveillance Process?', *ASEAN Economic Bulletin*, 18(1) (2001), 94 at 97.

[37] Gil, *ASEAN Towards the 21st Century: A Thirty-Year Review of the Association of Southeast Asian Nations*, pp. 147–69.

2.4 Facilitation

Quite apart from securing substantive or formal compliance, or clarifying the content of present or future obligations, a monitoring mechanism may also provide services to members that facilitate implementation.

First, a mechanism may provide technical expertise and knowledge to help countries to implement an agreement, especially those lacking sufficient resources.[38] This can be done directly by providing consultancy services and technical support. It can also be done indirectly by providing a platform for states parties to share experiences.

Secondly, a monitoring mechanism may seek to provide a public good or goods with a high positive externality. Macroeconomic surveillance and early warning mechanisms guarding against financial instability are examples of this, seeking to distribute information that is relevant to all parties though for reasons distinct from compliance per se.

A recent example of an important facilitative role is AMRO. The compliance function of AMRO was discussed earlier.[39] In terms of its facilitative role, AMRO was intended to support economic growth and stability in ASEAN+3 in two ways. First, the surveillance could warn countries of impending crises and hence aid management. Secondly, the additional crisis management capacity through potential currency swaps may attract investment. If investors believe that the

[38] Worapot Manupipatpong, 'The ASEAN Surveillance Process and the East Asian Monetary Fund', *ASEAN Economic Bulletin*, 19(1) (2002), 111 at 114; Ravenhill, 'Economic Cooperation'.
[39] See section 2.1.

mechanism is likely to function and stabilise countries during a crisis, they would be more willing to invest. As MAS Director Ravi Menon has stated:

> Regional safety net mechanisms – like the CMIM – will provide added assurance to markets that governments have the tools and resources to deal with the economic or financial challenges at hand. They can be more focused in surveillance, more timely in execution, and more contextual in policy prescription, providing balance to the multilateral approach.[40]

AMRO's success in this area will depend on the availability of resources and the willingness of countries to cooperate with information gathering. Here, the traditional criticism of the ASEAN Secretariat is that it lacks the financial and human resources to monitor economic developments. Given the involvement of the +3 countries, it is likely that AMRO would have a significantly larger budget. The Asian Development Bank (ADB) is also providing technical expertise to AMRO. In October 2011, AMRO had ten staff, though it was suggested that this would increase to twenty-one in 2012.[41]

AMRO will also need to obtain the cooperation of countries in order to gather information. The lack of willingness to share information is another problem that has hindered economic surveillance in ASEAN. AMRO intends

---

[40] Ravi Menon, 'Regional Safety Nets to Complement Global Safety Nets' (AMRO, Singapore, 31 January 2012).

[41] Wei Benhua, 'Speech by Mr Wei Benhua, AMRO Director' (AMRO, Singapore, 31 January 2012).

to send annual missions to all of the countries. It remains to be seen whether the initial favourable reception will continue.

Indeed, the facilitative purpose of monitoring seems to be applicable to many of the mechanisms examined in Chapter 1. In particular, the many situations in which notional monitoring mechanisms were established without budgets or formal powers seem to fit this category best, if they are to be regarded as more than purely symbolic. In the economic field, this might include agreements such as the 1977 Agreement on ASEAN Preferential Trading Arrangements,[42] the 1980 Basic Agreement on ASEAN Industrial Projects,[43] the 1995 ASEAN Customs Code of Conduct[44] and the 2009 Agreement on Trade in Goods with India.[45] In the political-security field, it would include the 2007 Declaration on Migrant Workers[46] and the 2009 AICHR.[47] In the socio-cultural area, the 1987 Resolution on Sustainable Development[48] might be counted as primarily facilitative.

A more interesting example may be the 1988 Post-Harvest Programme funded by Canada. The obligation to 'furnish the other [party] with such information as shall reasonably be requested' in particular might suggest the

---

[42] See section 1.1.1.1.
[43] See section 1.1.1.2.
[44] See section 1.1.1.6.
[45] See section 1.1.1.21.
[46] See section 1.2.4.2.
[47] See section 1.2.4.3.
[48] See section 1.3.2.2.

possibility of meaningful peer pressure to comply with the obligations undertaken, but in a development context may more accurately be seen as facilitative.[49] Similarly, the provisions in the three air services agreements of 2009 and 2010 concerning consultations would fit into this category.[50]

Finally, the general monitoring of integration in the three communities may be seen as facilitative – where it does not appear to be symbolic. This would apply to the facilitative monitoring of economic integration,[51] though in the political-security and socio-cultural spheres the monitoring may be seen as more symbolic. The Blueprints may be an exception to this, with an apparent interest in setting out a framework for the flow of information that should facilitate implementation.[52] Similarly, the ACPMS has allowed sharing of statistics that may facilitate implementation of other obligations.[53]

2.5 Symbolism

A final category of monitoring mechanisms may serve a primarily symbolic or political purpose. This may be as general as emphasising the unity of the organisation or be intended to show the importance attached to a particular

---

[49] See section 1.1.1.3.
[50] See section 1.1.1.23.
[51] See section 1.1.2.
[52] See sections 1.2.1.5, 1.3.1.2.
[53] See sections 1.1.2.2, 1.3.1.1.

issue. What distinguishes this purpose is that the key factor driving the monitoring mechanism is perception. Such a focus on perception – in particular the perception of unity – has historically been important within ASEAN. During the Cold War years in particular, and after the Asian financial crisis, ASEAN sought to be a stabilising force within the region.[54]

Indications that monitoring is being undertaken for purely symbolic reasons rather than even to facilitate implementation may include national reports that may not even be shared with other states parties. This was the case, for example, in some of the early steps towards human rights monitoring, such as the 2004 Declaration on the Elimination of Violence Against Women in the ASEAN Region.[55]

In other cases, vague reporting obligations to the ASEAN Secretariat without an obligation on the part of the Secretariat to report to anyone else may essentially be regarded as symbolic. This was the case, for example, for the 1996 ASEAN Industrial Cooperation Scheme,[56] the 2007 Mutual Recognition Arrangement on Architectural Services,[57] the 1976 and 2003 Declarations of ASEAN Concord,[58] the 1985 Agreement on the Conservation of

---

[54] Narine, *Explaining ASEAN: Regionalism in Southeast Asia*, pp. 13–22, 161–9.
[55] See section 1.2.4.1.
[56] See section 1.1.1.9.
[57] See section 1.1.1.17.
[58] See sections 1.2.1.1, 1.2.1.2.

Nature and Natural Resources[59] and the 2005 Agreement on Disaster Management and Emergency Response.[60]

In still other cases, provision for a periodic review by the relevant ministers at a scheduled meeting – as opposed to an obligation for some entity to report to that meeting – may be treated as symbolic. This would include the 2007 MOU with China on Sanitary and Phytosanitary Cooperation.[61]

Monitoring of the ongoing Thailand–Cambodia border dispute may be regarded as symbolic since the observers were not allowed into Thailand due, among other things, to disagreements over their terms of reference.[62] Similarly, the 2012 election observers in Myanmar were essentially a symbolic act to endorse Myanmar's transition to democracy.[63]

A final example of the symbolic purpose of monitoring may be seen even in mechanisms with more substantive purposes. A speech by Choi Jong Ku, Co-Chair of the ELDMB, suggests that there may be a political function behind AMRO as well:

> Our hopes are high that AMRO will not only serve as an organisation which monitors the regional macroeconomic status and assists CMIM Decision Making Body, but also develop into an internationally-recognised unit that will

[59] See section 1.3.2.1.
[60] See section 1.3.2.4.
[61] See section 1.1.1.16.
[62] See section 1.2.5.3.
[63] See section 1.2.5.4.

contribute to the global economy and show the world what Asia is all about.[64]

2.6 Conclusions

Having reviewed both the chronology as well as a rough typology of monitoring within ASEAN, three broad conclusions can be drawn.

The first is that monitoring of all types is becoming more common. It is now standard to have some kind of monitoring component to an agreement or MOU, even if the powers and resources of that mechanism are weak.

The second conclusion is that the willingness to accept more formal and compliance-focused monitoring has increased over time. This is true across all three communities, but most marked in respect of the increased activity in the economic community.

The third is that there is generally greater willingness to accept stronger monitoring regimes in the economic rather than political-security and socio-cultural contexts. That conclusion is further reinforced if one excludes the exceptional cases of monitoring in the security sphere that were not strictly ASEAN operations.

Using a simple conversion that attributes numerical values to the different forms of monitoring examined in this section, it is possible to plot the mechanisms graphically,

---

[64] JongKu Choi, 'Congratulatory Remarks by Deputy Minister JongKu Choi, Ministry of Strategy and Finance, Republic of Korea' (AMRO, Singapore, 31 January 2012).

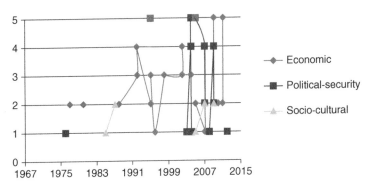

Figure 2.1 Monitoring of different ASEAN Community obligations (1 = symbolism, 2 = facilitation, 3 = interpretation, 4 = implementation, 5 = compliance)

illustrating, as in Figure 2.1, (a) the increased frequency with which monitoring mechanisms are being adopted, (b) the general trend towards stronger monitoring, and (c) the increased tendency to accept such obligations in the economic field in particular.

Such conclusions are not surprising, reflecting ASEAN's long-standing emphasis on economic cooperation, episodic demands for joint action on political and security matters, and the relative novelty of meaningful cooperation in the socio-cultural sphere.

Chapter 3

Typologies of Monitoring: A Toolkit

The preceding chapters have examined the evolution of monitoring in ASEAN and developed a taxonomy of purposes for which monitoring may be intended. This final chapter offers a toolkit for future monitoring exercises, drawing on ASEAN and other international experience.

Many factors will affect the institutional design of a monitoring mechanism, most obviously the purpose to be served but also the resources available. As we have seen, ASEAN's approach to monitoring has frequently been shaped also by wariness of exposing domestic activities to external scrutiny, and a more general preference for facilitating compliance rather than objectively assessing it in either a formal or substantive sense. Without taking a position on the desirability of different approaches, this chapter is intended to clarify the options available so that informed choices can be made about the appropriate model to adopt for a given situation. In practice, of course, design of a monitoring mechanism will often be governed by *supply* – that is, the willingness of states to subject themselves to monitoring – rather than *demand*. But for present purposes the intention is to highlight such choices so that there is at least clarity about the decisions that are being made.

Three preliminary points about the design of a monitoring regime should be made. The first concerns legal transplantation. There is, of course, value in learning from the experiences of other regions. But there are significant limits to what can be achieved by uncritically exporting mechanisms that work in one region to another, or drawing conclusions based on dubious comparisons between the needs and interests of members. A spectacular example of the limitation of such an approach to reforming institutions was the 'law and development' movement of the 1960s. This was an ambitious programme run by the US Agency for International Development, the Ford Foundation, and other private American donors seeking to reform the laws and judicial institutions of countries in Africa, Asia and Latin America. The programme generated hundreds of reports and articles. A decade later, however, leading academic participants and a former official at the Ford Foundation declared it a failure. Criticisms included the programme's over-reliance on exporting certain aspects of the US legal system – notably strategic litigation and activist judges – that were incompatible with the target countries.[1]

---

[1] David M. Trubek and Marc Galanter, 'Scholars in Self-Estrangement: Some Reflections on the Crisis in Law and Development', *Wisconsin Law Review*, 4 (1974), 1062; John H. Merryman, 'Comparative Law and Social Change: On the Origins, Style, Decline & Revival of the Law and Development Movement', *American Journal of Comparative Law*, 25 (1977), 457; James Gardner, *Legal Imperialism: American Lawyers and Foreign Aid in Latin America* (Madison: University of Wisconsin Press, 1980). Later assessments have been less negative, however, noting that law reform projects take many years to bear fruit and that the rise and fall of the movement may have been more connected to US domestic political issues in the period 1965–75 than with programmes on the ground in developing countries. Mary McClymont and Stephen Golub (eds.), *Many Roads to Justice: The Law-Related Work of Ford Foundation Grantees around the World* (New York: Ford Foundation, 2000); Brian Z.

This is true both at the regional level – comparisons, say, between ASEAN and the EU are to be drawn only with great caution – as well as at the level of domestic jurisdictions. Various monitoring regimes seek to import international standards into domestic laws and institutions. Such a regime will be most effective if there are compatible laws and institutions within those domestic regimes – and may be ineffective if there are not.[2]

A second preliminary point is that a monitoring mechanism does not need to be unified or monolithic. Assuming the purpose is to encourage compliance, monitoring should be demand- rather than supply-focused. That is, the approach may be different across sectors and indeed by country. This is particularly true with respect to ASEAN, where the very different natures of the economies of Member States mean that some will be more susceptible to certain forms of monitoring rather than others. Referring back to the problem of data collection, a basic issue may be the collection of statistical data – something significantly easier in Singapore than, say, Myanmar.

The third issue is the object of monitoring. This is meant both in the sense of the *purpose* of a mechanism – a

Tamanaha, 'The Lessons of Law-and-Development Studies', *American Journal of International Law*, 89 (1995), 470.

[2] See, e.g., Karen J. Alter and Laurence R. Helfer, 'The Andean Tribunal of Justice and its Interlocutors: Understanding Preliminary Reference Patterns in the Andean Community', *New York University Journal of International Law and Politics*, 41 (2009), 871 (discussing how the Andean Tribunal of Justice adopted preliminary reference procedures modelled on the European Court of Justice but with very different effects, attributable to the different ways in which the two institutions interact with the legal and administrative systems of their Member States).

topic considered in Chapter 2 – as well as the *subject matter* to be monitored. In particular, the object of monitoring may itself be a non-binding obligation. As Laurence Helfer has argued, however, even the monitoring of non-binding provisions can impact on behaviour by reducing the competitive advantage of those who do not take on such obligations; it raises the costs of cheating, and most importantly it provides a mechanism for domestic interest groups to challenge government practices that fall short of international standards.[3] In this way, monitoring may still be intended to encourage compliance, though in the sense of movement towards a shared goal rather than achievement of a concrete end.

This chapter seeks to clarify some of the key variables in monitoring mechanisms in the hope that it may guide future practice. Matters to be addressed include *who* performs the monitoring, *how* data are collected, *when* monitoring takes place, *what powers* are available to monitors, and the *transparency* of the monitoring process.

3.1 Who Monitors?

Assuming that the purpose and the subject matter of monitoring have been determined, a key question is who collects the data on compliance. There are at least nine possibilities. The intention here is only to sketch out the possibilities, though there is considerable scope for variation within each of the categories.

---

[3] Laurence R. Helfer, 'The Law and Politics of International Delegation: Monitoring Compliance with Unratified Treaties – The ILO Experience', *Law and Contemporary Problems*, 71 (2008), 193.

3.1.1 *Secretariat*

Monitoring by the secretariat of an organisation may provide a measure of objectivity, but its effectiveness depends on resources and political will. In the case of ASEAN, as we have seen, neither has been in strong supply throughout much of its history. That said, the vague but potentially broad powers given to the Secretary-General may suggest a greater role for the Secretariat in the future.[4]

3.1.2 *Independent Regional Mechanism*

Distinct from a secretariat, an independent regional mechanism may be created.[5] In NAFTA, for example, in addition to a Secretariat a Free Trade Commission was established to supervise the work of the committees and working groups created under the agreement, oversee any changes to the agreement and resolve disputes arising from the interpretation and application of the agreement.[6] Under the Andean Community of Nations (CAN)–Mercosur Agreements, an Administrative Commission was established and does its monitoring task through annual

---

[4] See Chapter 1, text accompanying notes 8–13.

[5] In limited contexts, this might include an independent tribunal, such as the advisory jurisdiction of the ICJ and ITLOS discussed in section 2.3. Note that the emphasis here is on monitoring rather than dispute resolution more generally.

[6] Frederick M. Abbott, 'Integration without Institutions: The NAFTA Mutation of the EC Model and the Future of the GATT Regime', *American Journal of Comparative Law*, 40(4) (1992), 917 at 933.

meetings.[7] Within ASEAN, the creation of AMRO in 2011 suggests a willingness to use such a mechanism, at least with respect to the ASEAN Economic Community.[8]

3.1.3 Regional Political Mechanism

A more common measure adopted in ASEAN is to leave notional monitoring to a gathering of government representatives at the regional level, such as the ASEAN Ministerial Meeting. When ministers with relevant portfolios are tasked with reviewing reports on compliance, this may serve as a serious monitoring regime – as in the case of the 1992 CEPT Scheme,[9] the 2002 MOU on Trans-ASEAN Gas,[10] the 2004 Agreement on Trade in Goods between ASEAN and China,[11] the 2007 MOU on the ASEAN Power Grid,[12] the 2009 Agreement on Investment between ASEAN and China,[13] the 2004 ASEAN Security Community Plan of Action,[14] the 2009 Declaration on the Roadmap for the ASEAN Community[15] and the 2007 ASEAN Convention on Counter Terrorism.[16] When foreign ministers are merely given notional oversight

[7]   Philippe de Lombaerde, Antoni Estevadeordal and Kati Suominen (eds.), *Governing Regional Integration for Development: Monitoring Experiences, Methods and Prospects* (Aldershot: Ashgate, 2008), p. 17.
[8]   See section 1.1.2.5.
[9]   See section 1.1.1.5.
[10] See section 1.1.1.13.
[11] See section 1.1.1.14.
[12] See section 1.1.1.18.
[13] See section 1.1.1.22.
[14] See section 1.2.1.3.
[15] See section 1.2.1.4.
[16] See section 1.2.3.1.

with no obligation to report to them on compliance, such 'monitoring' may be dismissed as largely symbolic.[17]

3.1.4 Self-Monitoring

Self-monitoring is particularly common when the subject matter is sensitive or resource constraints limit the possibility of external monitors. Both factors weighed heavily in ASEAN's early years: anything that might affect the domestic jurisdiction of members was regarded as sensitive, and in any case the Secretariat had little or no capacity to engage in its own monitoring. Such monitoring may be the most common form, ranging from compliance with human rights[18] to economic obligations[19] – both within ASEAN and internationally. A key question is what happens to the data so collected. This is particularly true of self-monitoring as the incentive to act on such data may be low.

3.1.5 Peer Monitoring

Peer monitoring may address issues of trust with respect to other parties' intentions or actions. In the late 1960s and early 1970s for example, arms limitations negotiations between the United States and the Soviet Union stalled when there was no agreement on a verification regime. On-site inspections were out of the question. Eventual agreement was reached in an unusual provision that committed each side not to interfere

[17] See section 2.5.
[18] See, e.g., section 1.2.4.1.
[19] See, e.g., section 1.1.1.17.

with the surveillance of its activities by the other, allowing the United States to spy on Soviet missiles and vice versa.[20]

No such mechanism exists within ASEAN, though it is possible that the regional political mechanisms described earlier could serve such a function if it were an opportunity to scrutinise the activities of other members.[21] This is the process effectively adopted in various human rights mechanisms, such as the Universal Periodic Review under the auspices of the UN Human Rights Council, and certain environmental agreements.[22] Another interesting model is the disinvestment practices of major sovereign investors such as Norway, based on assessments of human rights and environmental compliance of companies in which they own shares.[23]

3.1.6 Other International Organisations

In some cases, other international organisations may be assigned a monitoring role. Though not part of ASEAN's experience – unless one includes AMRO's ambiguous relationship with the IMF[24] – this arrangement has been used in

---

[20] Simon Chesterman, *One Nation under Surveillance: A New Social Contract to Defend Freedom without Sacrificing Liberty* (Oxford University Press, 2011), pp. 33–4.

[21] See section 3.1.3.

[22] See, e.g., Rob Milne, 'Multi-Party Monitoring in Ontario: Challenges and Emerging Solutions', *Environments*, 34(1) (2006), 11.

[23] See Simon Chesterman, 'The Turn to Ethics: Disinvestment from Multinational Corporations for Human Rights Violations – The Case of Norway's Sovereign Wealth Fund', *American University International Law Review*, 23 (2008), 577.

[24] See section 2.1.

the context of the Millennium Development Goals (MDGs). The annual MDG reports compile data collected by the UN system as well as the Inter-Parliamentary Union and the Organisation for Economic Co-operation and Development (OECD) among others.[25]

3.1.7 Civil Society

Civil society is an often-overlooked component of monitoring. A World Bank study highlighted the important monitoring role that civil society can play to support governance in developing countries in particular.[26] At the international level, the International Committee of the Red Cross occupies a unique space in which a notionally private association is given a formal role as a controlling authority under the Geneva Conventions.[27] Frequently, however, the monitoring role is self-appointed, with non-governmental organisations (NGOs) such as Human Rights Watch, Amnesty International and Freedom House issuing reports on the human rights records of states. Other prominent examples include Transparency International's Corruption Perception Index and the World Justice Project's Rule of Law Index.[28]

[25] *The Millennium Development Goals Report 2012* (New York: United Nations, 2012).

[26] Keith Mackay, *How to Build M&E Systems to Support Better Government* (Washington DC: World Bank Independent Evaluation Group, 2007), 13–15.

[27] See, e.g., Convention Relative to the Protection of Civilian Persons in Time of War (Fourth Geneva Convention), done at Geneva, 12 August 1949, art. 10.

[28] See generally Tullio Treves (ed.), *Civil Society, International Courts and Compliance Bodies* (The Hague: TMC Asser, 2005); Ulrich Beyerlin (ed.),

The role of civil society within ASEAN remains very much a work in progress, though much of this is focused on the self-appointed role of NGOs.[29] Other forms of civil society engagement that have historically been more palatable include the role of universities, such as the ASEAN University Network and Human Rights Education Network. Similarly, think tanks and research institutes can play a role in gathering data on compliance with ASEAN and other obligations. A further aspect of civil society that can play a role is traditional and new media, though these have not traditionally had significant impact on government policies around the region.[30]

3.1.8 Private Enterprises

In fields such as corporate social responsibility (CSR), an increasingly important role in monitoring has been essentially delegated to corporations.[31] This has long been the case with self-monitoring in respect of international labour standards,[32]

    Ensuring Compliance with Multilateral Environmental Agreements: A Dialogue Between Practitioners and Academia (Leiden: Nijhoff, 2006).

[29] See, e.g., Alan Collins, 'A People-Oriented ASEAN: A Door Ajar or Closed for Civil Society Organizations?', *Contemporary Southeast Asia*, 30(2) (2008), 313; Tan Hsien-Li, *ASEAN Intergovernmental Commission*, pp. 163–7.

[30] See, e.g., Cherian George, *Freedom from the Press: Journalism and State Power in Singapore* (Singapore: NUS Press, 2012).

[31] See, e.g., David Weissbrodt, 'Business and Human Rights', *University of Cincinnati Law Review*, 74 (2005), 55; Edwin M. Epstein, 'The Good Company: Rhetoric or Reality? Corporate Social Responsibility and Business Ethics Redux', *American Business Law Journal*, 44 (2007), 207.

[32] See, e.g., Erin Burnett and James Mahon, 'Monitoring Compliance with International Labor Standards', *Challenge*, 44(2) (2001), 51.

but through the Global Compact and John Ruggie's work on business and human rights it has become more sophisticated and, arguably, more influential.[33]

No such formal regime exists within ASEAN, though the ABF represents an interesting experiment, encouraging an active role by businesses in the region albeit in a very narrow area.[34] Among other things, the ABF states that the first of its objectives is to 'track and update AEC's accomplishments against AEC blueprint'.[35]

3.1.9 Individuals

A final category of potential monitors is individual citizens. Though often conflated with civil society, the idea here is that individuals may play a role in flagging potential problems in compliance. The most obvious example is where individuals are given standing to do so through mechanisms such as the First Optional Protocol to the ICCPR.[36] In addition, citizens may play a role in the context of civil society organisations as indicated earlier.[37] In some cases, they may be granted standing to bring litigation in the public interest, which may also serve as a form of monitoring of compliance with international obligations. In the United

---

[33] Simon Chesterman, 'Lawyers, Guns, and Money: The Governance of Business Activities in Conflict Zones', *Chicago Journal of International Law*, 11 (2011), 321.

[34] See section 2.3.

[35] See www.aseanbusinessforum.com/about.

[36] ICCPR, 16 December 1966, 999 UNTS 171, in force 23 March 1976.

[37] See section 3.1.7.

States, this is informally referred to as being a 'private attorney general'.[38]

Such practice does not seem to exist – at least, not yet – within ASEAN. Indeed, one of the interesting questions for the AICHR will be how it handles individual complaints. Though its terms of reference do not provide for it to receive such complaints, there is no explicit prohibition from doing so – an ambiguity that some have suggested may leave space for greater responsiveness to individuals.[39]

3.2 How Are Data Collected?

The question of how monitoring is conducted will frequently be tied closely to the identity of the monitor. An important distinction can be made between 'vertical' and 'horizontal' monitoring. 'Vertical' monitoring takes place in the context of a hierarchical relationship such as the role of an independent regional mechanism[40] or a regional political mechanism.[41] In such arrangements there is a literal accountability, in the sense that there is an obligation to provide an account to the supervising entity. 'Horizontal' monitoring assumes a relationship of equals, as in the case of

---

[38] See, e.g., Julie E. Steiner, 'Should "Substitute" Private Attorneys General Enforce Public Environmental Actions? Balancing the Costs and Benefits of the Contingency Fee Environmental Special Counsel Arrangement', *Santa Clara Law Review*, 51 (2011), 853; David Freeman Engstrom, 'Harnessing the Private Attorney General: Evidence from Qui Tam Litigation', *Columbia Law Review*, 112 (2012), 1244.

[39] Tan Hsien-Li, *ASEAN Intergovernmental Commission*, p. 161.

[40] See section 3.1.2.

[41] See section 3.1.3.

peer monitoring.[42] In some international organisations, monitoring by the secretariat might be considered a vertical relationship, but presumes the existence of supervisory powers granted to the secretariat. In the case of ASEAN, this would be a dubious presumption.[43]

A separate question is whether monitoring is active or passive. In the foregoing analysis, the emphasis has been on the activity of collecting data on compliance. This may be considered to be 'active' monitoring. It can be argued that the receipt of such data may itself be a form of 'passive' monitoring – indeed, the absence of a clear reporting line was used to justify the categorisation of certain monitoring mechanisms as largely 'symbolic'.[44] The effectiveness of such monitoring depends in turn upon whether there is any proactive consideration of the data so received. In sensitive areas such as human rights, for example, slow moves towards detailed discussion of country reports characterised the first decades of the human rights mechanisms that existed within the United Nations. Within the context of ASEAN, the tendency to avoid confrontation significantly limits this aspect of monitoring, though there appears to be some evidence of informal discussions leading to modest pressure as in the case of Myanmar's decision to forgo the ASEAN chair in 2006 – ostensibly 'so that it could focus on an internal process of reconciliation and democratisation',[45]

[42] See section 3.1.5.
[43] See section 3.1.1.
[44] See section 2.5.
[45] Susilo Bambang Yudhoyono, 'On Building the ASEAN Community: The Democratic Aspect' (ASEAN, Jakarta, 8 August 2005).

though in reality because of embarrassment over its human rights record.[46]

Monitoring may also be formal or informal. Generally, the more concrete the obligations, the more formal the monitoring should be, though again the identity of the monitors may be important. Examples of informal monitoring include the role played by civil society,[47] private enterprises[48] and individuals.[49]

3.3 When Does Monitoring Take Place?

The timing of monitoring may also be important. Within the political science literature, two broad theories of oversight are known as the 'police-patrol' and 'fire-alarm' models. In the former, a sample of activities is investigated with the aim of detecting and remedying problematic behaviour and, through this surveillance, discouraging it. In the latter, a system is put in place where interested groups are empowered to raise an alarm and thus set in motion a response. The authors who developed these models were focused on congressional oversight and sought to challenge conventional wisdom in the United States that denounced the legislature's neglect of its oversight responsibilities. They argued instead that Congress had implicitly chosen the more efficient

---

[46] Luz Baguioro, 'Asean Chair: Your Move, Myanmar; Asean Ministers Hopeful Yangon Will Step Aside', *Straits Times* (Singapore), 12 April 2005.

[47] See section 3.1.7.

[48] See section 3.1.8.

[49] See section 3.1.9.

fire-alarm model of reactive rather than centralised and continuous intervention.[50]

Within ASEAN, most reporting on compliance would notionally be described as 'active' in that it does not require a crisis to initiate monitoring. Yet for the most part, this takes the form of a reporting obligation or inclusion of a matter on a meeting agenda. In such cases, if the obligation to report is a periodic one in advance of a meeting, it would appear more likely to focus attention on implementation and compliance issues. Where there is merely a vague obligation to report but without a specified time frame, such monitoring was previously categorised as largely symbolic in nature.[51]

Some notable exceptions would include the 1988 Post-Harvest Programme, which allowed parties to request the furnishing of information;[52] the 1995 Nuclear-Weapon-Free Zone Treaty, which allowed parties to request 'clarifications' of one another;[53] and the 2009 Air Services Agreements, which allowed for consultations to be initiated at the request of one of the parties.[54]

3.4 What Powers Do Monitors Have?

The power of monitors is a largely hypothetical topic within the context of ASEAN. Even in situations where the

---

[50] Mathew D. McCubbins and Thomas Schwartz, 'Congressional Oversight Overlooked: Police Patrols versus Fire Alarms', *American Journal of Political Science*, 28 (1984), 165 at 166–76.

[51] See section 2.5.

[52] See section 1.1.1.3.

[53] See section 1.2.2.1.

[54] See section 1.1.1.23.

monitoring is by a motivated entity with the purpose of ensuring substantive compliance, there are no coercive powers associated with monitoring. Instead, the 'ASEAN Way' of consultation and consensus would seem to be dominant.[55]

Nevertheless, in addition to the possibility of shaming discussed in the next section,[56] a range of non-coercive measures is available to encourage compliance with the obligation to monitor (quite apart from any obligation to comply with the underlying obligation being monitored). These include technical assistance linked with monitoring, ensuring the technical expertise and political independence of monitors (making it less likely that they will be subject to regulatory capture),[57] through adoption of formal processes with red flags raised by non-compliance, to notification procedures when monitoring deadlines are missed.[58]

Moving still further into the realm of hypothesis, as far as ASEAN is concerned, some monitoring regimes do embrace coercive measures to deal with the failure to conduct monitoring as required. The Convention on International Trade in Endangered Species of Wild Fauna and Flora

---

[55] See section 2.1.
[56] See section 3.5.
[57] See, e.g., Jean-Jacques Laffont and Jean Tirole, 'The Politics of Government Decision-Making: A Theory of Regulatory Capture', *Quarterly Journal of Economics*, 106 (1991), 1089.
[58] Cf. Rosalind Reeve, 'The Convention on International Trade in Endangered Species of Wild Fauna and Flora (CITES)', in Geir Ulfstein (ed.), *Making Treaties Work: Human Rights, Environment and Arms Control* (Cambridge University Press, 2007), pp. 148–52.

(CITES), for example, now provides that failure to report as required for three years in a row could lead to a ban on trade in CITES-listed species.[59]

3.5 How Transparent Is the Mechanism?

A final consideration is the transparency of monitoring. As indicated earlier, this can be an important means of encouraging – as opposed to coercing – compliance with the monitoring obligations.[60] Within ASEAN, such monitoring as is meant to take place often does so out of the public eye. Among other things, that goes to explain the decision in this study to focus on the institutional design of monitoring rather than an empirical examination of its effectiveness in practice.[61]

Such a lack of transparency is not limited to ASEAN and has been the subject of criticism. In environmental law, for example, the 1992 Rio Declaration stated that environmental issues are best handled with the participation of all concerned citizens, which in turn requires access to information.[62] More progress has, again, been made in the

---

[59] Resolution Conf. 11.17 (Rev. CoP16), 'National Reports' (Convention on International Trade in Endangered Species of Wild Fauna and Flora (CITES), 2004); Reeve, 'Convention on International Trade', pp. 144–5.

[60] See section 3.4.

[61] See the Introduction.

[62] Rio Declaration on Environment and Development, 12 August 1992, UN Doc. A/CONF.151/26 (Vol. 1), Annex I, Principle 10. See Attila Tanzi and Cesare Pitea, 'Non-Compliance Mechanisms: Lessons Learned and the Way Forward', in Tullio Treves et al. (eds.), *Non-Compliance Procedures and Mechanisms and the Effectiveness of International Environmental Agreements* (The Hague: T.M.C. Asser Press, 2009), pp. 576–7.

economic field with relative transparency of economic monitoring, including through the publication of statistics.[63]
There may be special cases in which it is necessary to keep
certain information confidential, such as matters that are
commercially sensitive or relate to national security. But
even in such areas it has generally been possible and desirable
to increase transparency, as seen in the various efforts to
outlaw biological and chemical weapons, and to restrict the
testing and acquisition of nuclear weapons.[64]

Moving forward, demands for transparency in the
embryonic governance structures of ASEAN are certain to
grow. As the global administrative law project has documented,
transparency in decision-making and access to information
are both an increasingly common practice and an emerging
norm at the global level.[65] Within ASEAN, much as domestic
governance structures have haltingly moved towards greater
transparency, such moves at the ASEAN level may come
to be seen as enhancing both the legitimacy as well as the
effectiveness of the regimes created under its auspices.[66]

---

[63] See section 2.4.

[64] Thilo Marauhn, 'Dispute Resolution, Compliance Control and
Enforcement of International Arms Control Law', in Ulfstein (ed.),
Making Treaties Work: Human Rights, Environment and Arms Control.

[65] Benedict Kingsbury, Nico Krisch and Richard B. Stewart, 'The
Emergence of Global Administrative Law', *Law and Contemporary
Problems*, 68 (2005), 15 at 37–9; Simon Chesterman, 'Globalization Rules:
Accountability, Power, and the Prospects for Global Administrative
Law', *Global Governance*, 14 (2008), 39.

[66] As in many other areas, however, this raises questions of whether
ASEAN will be given resources to publish data in a timely and accessible
fashion.

Conclusion

ASEAN remains a work in progress. The bold steps taken to create the ASEAN Community by 2015 are a radical departure from the early beginnings of ASEAN as a periodic meeting of foreign ministers. Achieving the goals that have been set presumes, first, that achieving those goals is in fact the intention. Past experience supports such cynicism, with estimates that only 30 per cent of past ASEAN obligations have ever been implemented.[1]

Since the adoption of the Charter, however, there appears to have been a significant increase in the acceptance of binding obligations. As Chapter 1 showed, the evolution – a term chosen carefully as it suggests experimentation and natural selection rather than intelligent design – of monitoring mechanisms in the various areas of ASEAN moved in fits and starts. Predictably, far more was done in the economic sphere but there were notable exceptions to the general wariness of opening up political questions to external scrutiny, with respect to shared problems such as haze and clear threats such as nuclear weapons.

Chapter 2 then developed a lens through which to view this greater willingness to accept monitoring over time, which was accompanied by a willingness for such monitoring to focus on compliance and implementation, rather than simply to coordinate interpretation of an obligation, facilitate

---

[1] See Chapter 1, note 15.

compliance or be a largely symbolic gesture. Again, predictably, this trend was clearest with respect to the Economic Community.

Assuming these trends continue, more attention may be paid to designing monitoring mechanisms to encourage substantive compliance. To this end, Chapter 3 sought to clarify some of the options available. These include the identity of monitors and their methodology, the timing of monitoring and the powers available to ensure that it takes place, as well as issues of transparency.

Barriers remain. The resources available to ASEAN continue to be a fraction of what any comparable regional organisation has at its disposal. ASEAN's entire budget for 2012 was US$15.8 million, while its members contributed approximately US$13.4 million to the WTO budget in the same year.[2] This imposes hard constraints on the capacity of the Secretariat in particular to play a meaningful role. Effective monitoring costs money. Yet, as we have seen, there are also costs associated with the failure to monitor.

The willingness to give ASEAN meaningful resources and a degree of independence is linked to changes in the second barrier: the political resistance to binding obligations generally. Member States have clearly relaxed their position on this in recent years, in part through rising comfort levels with international obligations and also through the necessity of confronting collective action problems. The work of the National University of Singapore's *Integration Through Law*

---

[2] All ASEAN states are now members of the WTO, with Laos joining in February 2013.

project, of which this book is a part, focuses on the role of law and the rule of law in regional integration – both reflecting and perhaps contributing to that new sensibility.

It remains to be seen whether these trends herald a more measured approach to decision-making in ASEAN in which commitments are made only when there is an intention to be bound, rather than as part of a shared aspiration. In the case of the three communities, however, such aspirations served the important purpose of setting ambitious goals to be achieved by 2015. Monitoring progress towards those goals may yet see ASEAN move from community to compliance.

EXECUTIVE SUMMARY

For most of its history, ASEAN reflected the wariness shown by many Asian states towards international organisations with binding obligations. In the past decade, however, ASEAN has undergone a transformation from a periodic meeting of ministers to setting ambitious goals of becoming an ASEAN Community by 2015. ASEAN has positioned itself at the centre of Asian regionalism through hub and spoke arrangements with China, India, Korea and Japan and is arguably the most important Asian international organisation in the history of the continent.

An important tension in this transformation is the question of whether the 'ASEAN Way' – defined by consultation and consensus, rather than enforceable obligations – is consistent with the establishment of a community governed by law. The National University of Singapore's *Integration Through Law* (*ITL*) project takes seriously the ASEAN claim to desire compliance with the various obligations that are the foundation of these new communities.

An important part of any compliance regime is the knowledge of what steps towards compliance have in fact been taken. Such knowledge presumes the collection of data on compliance, either for self-assessment or evaluative purposes.

The collection of those data is referred to here as 'monitoring'. The term embraces any institution, process, or practice (including informal practices) that gathers or shares information about whether or to what extent an ASEAN obligation has been complied with, in the sense of substantive compliance, or implemented, in the sense of formal compliance.

A survey of ASEAN agreements, however, reveals other apparent purposes for monitoring. In addition to assessing substantive and formal compliance (described here as *compliance sensu stricto* and *implementation* respectively), monitoring may provide an authoritative *interpretation* of the content of an obligation or the framework for taking on future obligations. A fourth purpose of monitoring may be the *facilitation* of long-term implementation through such measures as confidence-building and technology transfers. A fifth purpose may be purely *symbolic*: certain monitoring mechanisms are best understood as an expression of unity or of seriousness about an issue, rather than an intention to follow through on binding commitments.

The survey reveals a clear increase in recourse to monitoring over time, and more willingness for that monitoring to focus on substantive compliance or implementation, rather than coordinating interpretation, facilitation or serving symbolic purposes. This trend is clearest in the economic sphere but is broadly consistent with the adoption of the ASEAN Charter in 2007 and the goal of creating an ASEAN Community by 2015. It is reasonable to conclude that more monitoring will correlate with greater respect for and implementation of the relevant agreements.

Two barriers remain. The first is the resources available to ASEAN itself, which continue to be a fraction of what any comparable regional organisation has at its disposal. This imposes hard constraints on the capacity of the Secretariat to play a meaningful role. Effective monitoring costs money. But there are costs associated with the failure to monitor also.

Secondly, the Member States of ASEAN have historically been resistant to binding obligations generally. The failure to establish meaningful monitoring mechanisms in the first decades of ASEAN was not accidental – indeed, it is arguable that frequently there was no intention to follow through on obligations at all. That position has changed in recent years, however, in part through rising comfort levels with international obligations in general and the necessity of confronting specific collective action problems in particular.

It remains to be seen whether these trends herald a more measured approach to decision-making in ASEAN – in which commitments are made only when there is an intention to be bound, rather than as part of a shared aspiration. In the case of the three communities, however, such aspirations served the important purpose of setting ambitious goals to be achieved by 2015. Moving forward, monitoring progress towards those goals may yet see ASEAN move from community to compliance.

Appendices

1 The ASEAN Declaration (1967)

Adopted by the Foreign Ministers at the 1st ASEAN Ministerial Meeting in Bangkok, Thailand on 8 August 1967

The Presidium Minister for Political Affairs / Minister for Foreign Affairs of Indonesia, the Deputy Prime Minister of Malaysia, the Secretary of Foreign Affairs of the Philippines, the Minister for Foreign Affairs of Singapore and the Minister of Foreign Affairs of Thailand:

MINDFUL	of the existence of mutual interests and common problems among countries of South-East Asia and convinced of the need to strengthen further the existing bonds of regional solidarity and cooperation;
DESIRING	to establish a firm foundation for common action to promote regional cooperation in South-East Asia in the spirit of equality and partnership and thereby contribute towards peace, progress and prosperity in the region;

CONSCIOUS that in an increasingly interdependent world, the cherished ideals of peace, freedom, social justice and economic well-being are best attained by fostering good understanding, good neighbourliness and meaningful cooperation among the countries of the region already bound together by ties of history and culture;

CONSIDERING that the countries of South-East Asia share a primary responsibility for strengthening the economic and social stability of the region and ensuring their peaceful and progressive national development, and that they are determined to ensure their stability and security from external interference in any form or manifestation in order to preserve their national identities in accordance with the ideals and aspirations of their peoples;

AFFIRMING that all foreign bases are temporary and remain only with the expressed concurrence of the countries concerned and are not intended to be used directly or indirectly to subvert the national independence and freedom of States in the area or prejudice the orderly processes of their national development;

DO HEREBY DECLARE:

FIRST, the establishment of an Association for Regional Cooperation among the countries of South-East Asia to be known as the Association of South-East Asian Nations (ASEAN).

SECOND, that the aims and purposes of the Association shall be:

1. To accelerate the economic growth, social progress and cultural development in the region through joint endeavours in the spirit of equality and partnership in order to strengthen the foundation for a prosperous and peaceful community of South-East Asian Nations;
2. To promote regional peace and stability through abiding respect for justice and the rule of law in the relationship among countries of the region and adherence to the principles of the United Nations Charter;
3. To promote active collaboration and mutual assistance on matters of common interest in the economic, social, cultural, technical, scientific and administrative fields;

4. To provide assistance to each other in the form of training and research facilities in the educational, professional, technical and administrative spheres;

5. To collaborate more effectively for the greater utilisation of their agriculture and industries, the expansion of their trade, including the study of the problems of international commodity trade, the improvement of their transportation and communications facilities and the raising of the living standards of their peoples;

6. To promote South-East Asian studies;

7. To maintain close and beneficial cooperation with existing international and regional organisations with similar aims and purposes, and explore all avenues for even closer cooperation among themselves.

THIRD, that to carry out these aims and purposes, the following machinery shall be established:

(a) Annual Meeting of Foreign Ministers, which shall be by rotation and referred to as ASEAN Ministerial Meeting. Special Meetings of Foreign Ministers may be convened as required.

(b) A Standing Committee, under the chairmanship of the Foreign Minister of the host country or his representative and having as its members the accredited Ambassadors of the other member countries, to carry on the work of the Association in between Meetings of Foreign Ministers.

(c) Ad-Hoc Committees and Permanent Committees of specialists and officials on specific subjects.

(d) A National Secretariat in each member country to carry out the work of the Association on behalf of that country and to service the Annual or Special Meetings of Foreign Ministers, the Standing Committee and such other committees as may hereafter be established.

FOURTH, that the Association is open for participation to all States in the South-East Asian Region subscribing to the aforementioned aims, principles and purposes.

FIFTH, that the Association represents the collective will of the nations of South-East Asia to bind themselves together in friendship and cooperation and, through joint efforts and sacrifices, secure for their peoples and for posterity the blessings of peace, freedom and prosperity.

DONE in Bangkok on the Eighth Day of August in the Year One Thousand Nine Hundred and Sixty-Seven.

For the Republic of Indonesia: **ADAM MALIK**, Presidium Minister for Political Affairs Minister for Foreign Affairs

For Malaysia: **TUN ABDUL RAZAK BIN HUSSEIN**, Deputy Prime Minister and Minister of Defence and Minister of National Development

For the Republic of the Philippines: **MARCISO RAMOS**, Secretary of Foreign Affairs

For the Republic of Singapore: **S. RAJARATNAM**, Minister of Foreign Affairs

For the Kingdom of Thailand: **THANAT KHOMAN**, Minister of Foreign Affairs.

2 Charter of the Association of Southeast Asian Nations (2007)

Adopted by the Heads of State/Government at the 13th ASEAN Summit in Singapore on 20 November 2007

Preamble

WE, THE PEOPLES of the Member States of the Association of Southeast Asian Nations (ASEAN), as represented by the Heads of State or Government of Brunei Darussalam, the Kingdom of Cambodia, the Republic of Indonesia, the Lao People's Democratic Republic, Malaysia, the Union of Myanmar, the Republic of the Philippines, the Republic of Singapore, the Kingdom of Thailand and the Socialist Republic of Viet Nam;

NOTING with satisfaction the significant achieve-ments and expansion of ASEAN since its establishment in Bangkok through the promulgation of the ASEAN Declaration;

RECALLING the decisions to establish an ASEAN Charter in the Vientiane Action Programme, the Kuala Lumpur Declaration on the Establishment of the ASEAN Charter and the Cebu Declaration on the Blueprint of the ASEAN Charter;

MINDFUL of the existence of mutual interests and interdependence among the peoples and Member States of ASEAN which are bound by geography, common objectives and shared destiny;

INSPIRED by and united under One Vision, One Identity and One Caring and Sharing Community;

UNITED by a common desire and collective will to live in a region of lasting peace, security and stability, sustained economic growth, shared prosperity and social progress, and to promote our vital interests, ideals and aspirations;

RESPECTING the fundamental importance of amity and cooperation, and the principles of sovereignty, equality, territorial integrity, non-interference, consensus and unity in diversity;

ADHERING to the principles of democracy, the rule of law and good governance, respect for and protection of human rights and fundamental freedoms;

RESOLVED to ensure sustainable development for the benefit of present and future generations and to place the well-being, livelihood and welfare of the peoples at the centre of the ASEAN community building process;

CONVINCED of the need to strengthen existing bonds of regional solidarity to realise an ASEAN Community that is politically cohesive, economically integrated and socially responsible in order to effectively respond to current and future challenges and opportunities;

COMMITTED to intensifying community building through enhanced regional cooperation and integration, in particular by establishing an ASEAN Community comprising the ASEAN Security Community, the ASEAN Economic Community and the ASEAN Socio-Cultural Community, as provided for in the Bali Declaration of ASEAN Concord II;

HEREBY DECIDE to establish, through this Charter, the legal and institutional framework for ASEAN;

AND TO THIS END, the Heads of State or Government of the Member States of ASEAN, assembled in Singapore on the historic occasion of the 40th anniversary of the founding of ASEAN, have agreed to this Charter.

Chapter I Purposes and Principles

Article 1 Purposes

The Purposes of ASEAN are:

1. To maintain and enhance peace, security and stability and further strengthen peace-oriented values in the region;
2. To enhance regional resilience by promoting greater political, security, economic and socio-cultural cooperation;
3. To preserve Southeast Asia as a Nuclear Weapon-Free Zone and free of all other weapons of mass destruction;
4. To ensure that the peoples and Member States of ASEAN live in peace with the world at large in a just, democratic and harmonious environment;
5. To create a single market and production base which is stable, prosperous, highly competitive and economically integrated with effective facilitation for trade and investment in which there is free flow of goods, services and investment; facilitated movement of business persons, professionals, talents and labour; and freer flow of capital;
6. To alleviate poverty and narrow the development gap within ASEAN through mutual assistance and cooperation;

7. To strengthen democracy, enhance good governance and the rule of law, and to promote and protect human rights and fundamental freedoms, with due regard to the rights and responsibilities of the Member States of ASEAN;

8. To respond effectively, in accordance with the principle of comprehensive security, to all forms of threats, transnational crimes and transboundary challenges;

9. To promote sustainable development so as to ensure the protection of the region's environment, the sustainability of its natural resources, the preservation of its cultural heritage and the high quality of life of its peoples;

10. To develop human resources through closer cooperation in education and life-long learning, and in science and technology, for the empowerment of the peoples of ASEAN and for the strengthening of the ASEAN Community;

11. To enhance the well-being and livelihood of the peoples of ASEAN by providing them with equitable access to opportunities for human development, social welfare and justice;

12. To strengthen cooperation in building a safe, secure and drug-free environment for the peoples of ASEAN;

13. To promote a people-oriented ASEAN in which all sectors of society are encouraged to participate in, and benefit from, the process of ASEAN integration and community building;

14. To promote an ASEAN identity through the fostering of greater awareness of the diverse culture and heritage of the region; and

15. To maintain the centrality and proactive role of ASEAN as the primary driving force in its relations and cooperation with its external partners in a regional architecture that is open, transparent and inclusive.

Article 2 Principles

1. In pursuit of the Purposes stated in Article 1, ASEAN and its Member States reaffirm and adhere to the fundamental principles contained in the declarations, agreements, conventions, concords, treaties and other instruments of ASEAN.

2. ASEAN and its Member States shall act in accordance with the following Principles:

   (a) respect for the independence, sovereignty, equality, territorial integrity and national identity of all ASEAN Member States;

   (b) shared commitment and collective responsibility in enhancing regional peace, security and prosperity;

   (c) renunciation of aggression and of the threat or use of force or other actions in any manner inconsistent with international law;

   (d) reliance on peaceful settlement of disputes;

   (e) non-interference in the internal affairs of ASEAN Member States;

   (f) respect for the right of every Member State to lead its national existence free from external interference, subversion and coercion;

   (g) enhanced consultations on matters seriously affecting the common interest of ASEAN;

   (h) adherence to the rule of law, good governance, the principles of democracy and constitutional government;

   (i) respect for fundamental freedoms, the promotion and protection of human rights, and the promotion of social justice;

(j) upholding the United Nations Charter and international law, including international humanitarian law, subscribed to by ASEAN Member States;

(k) abstention from participation in any policy or activity, including the use of its territory, pursued by any ASEAN Member State or non-ASEAN State or any non-State actor, which threatens the sovereignty, territorial integrity or political and economic stability of ASEAN Member States;

(l) respect for the different cultures, languages and religions of the peoples of ASEAN, while emphasising their common values in the spirit of unity in diversity;

(m) the centrality of ASEAN in external political, economic, social and cultural relations while remaining actively engaged, outward-looking, inclusive and non-discriminatory; and

(n) adherence to multilateral trade rules and ASEAN's rules-based regimes for effective implementation of economic commitments and progressive reduction towards elimination of all barriers to regional economic integration, in a market-driven economy.

Chapter II Legal Personality

Article 3 Legal Personality of ASEAN

ASEAN, as an inter-governmental organisation, is hereby conferred legal personality.

Chapter III Membership

Article 4 Member States

The Member States of ASEAN are Brunei Darussalam, the Kingdom of Cambodia, the Republic of Indonesia, the Lao People's Democratic Republic, Malaysia, the Union of Myanmar, the Republic of the Philippines, the Republic of Singapore, the Kingdom of Thailand and the Socialist Republic of Viet Nam.

Article 5 Rights and Obligations

1. Member States shall have equal rights and obligations under this Charter.
2. Member States shall take all necessary measures, including the enactment of appropriate domestic legislation, to effectively implement the provisions of this Charter and to comply with all obligations of membership.
3. In the case of a serious breach of the Charter or noncompliance, the matter shall be referred to Article 20.

Article 6 Admission of New Members

1. The procedure for application and admission to ASEAN shall be prescribed by the ASEAN Coordinating Council.
2. Admission shall be based on the following criteria:
    (a) location in the recognised geographical region of Southeast Asia;
    (b) recognition by all ASEAN Member States;
    (c) agreement to be bound and to abide by the Charter; and

(d) ability and willingness to carry out the obligations of Membership.

3. Admission shall be decided by consensus by the ASEAN Summit, upon the recommendation of the ASEAN Coordinating Council.

4. An applicant State shall be admitted to ASEAN upon signing an Instrument of Accession to the Charter.

Chapter IV Organs

Article 7 ASEAN Summit

1. The ASEAN Summit shall comprise the Heads of State or Government of the Member States.

2. The ASEAN Summit shall:

   (a) be the supreme policy-making body of ASEAN;

   (b) deliberate, provide policy guidance and take decisions on key issues pertaining to the realisation of the objectives of ASEAN, important matters of interest to Member States and all issues referred to it by the ASEAN Coordinating Council, the ASEAN Community Councils and ASEAN Sectoral Ministerial Bodies;

   (c) instruct the relevant Ministers in each of the Councils concerned to hold ad hoc inter-Ministerial meetings, and address important issues concerning ASEAN that cut across the Community Councils. Rules of procedure for such meetings shall be adopted by the ASEAN Coordinating Council;

(d) address emergency situations affecting ASEAN by taking appropriate actions;

(e) decide on matters referred to it under Chapters VII and VIII;

(f) authorise the establishment and the dissolution of Sectoral Ministerial Bodies and other ASEAN institutions; and

(g) appoint the Secretary-General of ASEAN, with the rank and status of Minister, who will serve with the confidence and at the pleasure of the Heads of State or Government upon the recommendation of the ASEAN Foreign Ministers Meeting.

3. ASEAN Summit Meetings shall be:

(a) held twice annually, and be hosted by the Member State holding the ASEAN Chairmanship; and

(b) convened, whenever necessary, as special or ad hoc meetings to be chaired by the Member State holding the ASEAN Chairmanship, at venues to be agreed upon by ASEAN Member States.

Article 8 ASEAN Coordinating Council

1. The ASEAN Coordinating Council shall comprise the ASEAN Foreign Ministers and meet at least twice a year.

2. The ASEAN Coordinating Council shall:

(a) prepare the meetings of the ASEAN Summit;

(b) coordinate the implementation of agreements and decisions of the ASEAN Summit;

(c) coordinate with the ASEAN Community Councils to enhance policy coherence, efficiency and cooperation among them;

(d) coordinate the reports of the ASEAN Community Councils to the ASEAN Summit;

(e) consider the annual report of the Secretary-General on the work of ASEAN;

(f) consider the report of the Secretary-General on the functions and operations of the ASEAN Secretariat and other relevant bodies;

(g) approve the appointment and termination of the Deputy Secretaries-General upon the recommendation of the Secretary-General; and

(h) undertake other tasks provided for in this Charter or such other functions as may be assigned by the ASEAN Summit.

3. The ASEAN Coordinating Council shall be supported by the relevant senior officials.

Article 9   ASEAN Community Councils

1. The ASEAN Community Councils shall comprise the ASEAN Political-Security Community Council, ASEAN Economic Community Council, and ASEAN Socio-Cultural Community Council.

2. Each ASEAN Community Council shall have under its purview the relevant ASEAN Sectoral Ministerial Bodies.

3. Each Member State shall designate its national representation for each ASEAN Community Council meeting.

4. In order to realise the objectives of each of the three pillars of the ASEAN Community, each ASEAN Community Council shall:

   (a) ensure the implementation of the relevant decisions of the ASEAN Summit;

   (b) coordinate the work of the different sectors under its purview, and on issues which cut across the other Community Councils; and

   (c) submit reports and recommendations to the ASEAN Summit on matters under its purview.

5. Each ASEAN Community Council shall meet at least twice a year and shall be chaired by the appropriate Minister from the Member State holding the ASEAN Chairmanship.

6. Each ASEAN Community Council shall be supported by the relevant senior officials.

Article 10 ASEAN Sectoral Ministerial Bodies

1. ASEAN Sectoral Ministerial Bodies shall:

   (a) function in accordance with their respective established mandates;

   (b) implement the agreements and decisions of the ASEAN Summit under their respective purview;

   (c) strengthen cooperation in their respective fields in support of ASEAN integration and community building; and

   (d) submit reports and recommendations to their respective Community Councils.

2. Each ASEAN Sectoral Ministerial Body may have under its purview the relevant senior officials and subsidiary bodies

to undertake its functions as contained in Annex 1. The Annex may be updated by the Secretary-General of ASEAN upon the recommendation of the Committee of Permanent Representatives without recourse to the provision on Amendments under this Charter.

Article 11 Secretary-General of ASEAN and ASEAN Secretariat

1. The Secretary-General of ASEAN shall be appointed by the ASEAN Summit for a non-renewable term of office of five years, selected from among nationals of the ASEAN Member States based on alphabetical rotation, with due consideration to integrity, capability and professional experience, and gender equality.

2. The Secretary-General shall:
   (a) carry out the duties and responsibilities of this high office in accordance with the provisions of this Charter and relevant ASEAN instruments, protocols and established practices;
   (b) facilitate and monitor progress in the implementation of ASEAN agreements and decisions, and submit an annual report on the work of ASEAN to the ASEAN Summit;
   (c) participate in meetings of the ASEAN Summit, the ASEAN Community Councils, the ASEAN Coordinating Council, and ASEAN Sectoral Ministerial Bodies and other relevant ASEAN meetings;
   (d) present the views of ASEAN and participate in meetings with external parties in accordance with approved policy guidelines and mandate given to the Secretary-General; and

(e) recommend the appointment and termination of the Deputy Secretaries-General to the ASEAN Coordinating Council for approval.

3. The Secretary-General shall also be the Chief Administrative Officer of ASEAN.

4. The Secretary-General shall be assisted by four Deputy Secretaries-General with the rank and status of Deputy Ministers. The Deputy Secretaries-General shall be accountable to the Secretary-General in carrying out their functions.

5. The four Deputy Secretaries-General shall be of different nationalities from the Secretary-General and shall come from four different ASEAN Member States.

6. The four Deputy Secretaries-General shall comprise:

(a) two Deputy Secretaries-General who will serve a non-renewable term of three years, selected from among nationals of the ASEAN Member States based on alphabetical rotation, with due consideration to integrity, qualifications, competence, experience and gender equality; and

(b) two Deputy Secretaries-General who will serve a term of three years, which may be renewed for another three years. These two Deputy Secretaries-General shall be openly recruited based on merit.

7. The ASEAN Secretariat shall comprise the Secretary-General and such staff as may be required.

8. The Secretary-General and the staff shall:

(a) uphold the highest standards of integrity, efficiency, and competence in the performance of their duties;

(b) not seek or receive instructions from any government or external party outside of ASEAN; and

(c) refrain from any action which might reflect on their position as ASEAN Secretariat officials responsible only to ASEAN.

9. Each ASEAN Member State undertakes to respect the exclusively ASEAN character of the responsibilities of the Secretary-General and the staff, and not to seek to influence them in the discharge of their responsibilities.

Article 12 Committee of Permanent Representatives to ASEAN

1. Each ASEAN Member State shall appoint a Permanent Representative to ASEAN with the rank of Ambassador based in Jakarta.

2. The Permanent Representatives collectively constitute a Committee of Permanent Representatives, which shall:

(a) support the work of the ASEAN Community Councils and ASEAN Sectoral Ministerial Bodies;

(b) coordinate with ASEAN National Secretariats and other ASEAN Sectoral Ministerial Bodies;

(c) liaise with the Secretary-General of ASEAN and the ASEAN Secretariat on all subjects relevant to its work;

(d) facilitate ASEAN cooperation with external partners; and

(e) perform such other functions as may be determined by the ASEAN Coordinating Council.

Article 13 ASEAN National Secretariats

Each ASEAN Member State shall establish an ASEAN National Secretariat which shall:

(a) serve as the national focal point;

(b) be the repository of information on all ASEAN matters at the national level;

(c) coordinate the implementation of ASEAN decisions at the national level;

(d) coordinate and support the national preparations of ASEAN meetings;

(e) promote ASEAN identity and awareness at the national level; and

(f) contribute to ASEAN community building.

Article 14 ASEAN Human Rights Body

1. In conformity with the purposes and principles of the ASEAN Charter relating to the promotion and protection of human rights and fundamental freedoms, ASEAN shall establish an ASEAN human rights body.

2. This ASEAN human rights body shall operate in accordance with the terms of reference to be determined by the ASEAN Foreign Ministers Meeting.

Article 15 ASEAN Foundation

1. The ASEAN Foundation shall support the Secretary-General of ASEAN and collaborate with the relevant

ASEAN bodies to support ASEAN community building by promoting greater awareness of the ASEAN identity, people-to-people interaction, and close collaboration among the business sector, civil society, academia and other stakeholders in ASEAN.

2. The ASEAN Foundation shall be accountable to the Secretary-General of ASEAN, who shall submit its report to the ASEAN Summit through the ASEAN Coordinating Council.

Chapter V Entities Associated with ASEAN

Article 16 Entities Associated with ASEAN

1. ASEAN may engage with entities which support the ASEAN Charter, in particular its purposes and principles. These associated entities are listed in Annex 2.

2. Rules of procedure and criteria for engagement shall be prescribed by the Committee of Permanent Representatives upon the recommendation of the Secretary-General of ASEAN.

3. Annex 2 may be updated by the Secretary-General of ASEAN upon the recommendation of the Committee of Permanent Representatives without recourse to the provision on Amendments under this Charter.

Chapter VI Immunities and Privileges

Article 17 Immunities and Privileges of ASEAN

1. ASEAN shall enjoy in the territories of the Member States such immunities and privileges as are necessary for the fulfilment of its purposes.
2. The immunities and privileges shall be laid down in separate agreements between ASEAN and the host Member State.

Article 18 Immunities and Privileges of the Secretary-General of ASEAN and Staff of the ASEAN Secretariat

1. The Secretary-General of ASEAN and staff of the ASEAN Secretariat participating in official ASEAN activities or representing ASEAN in the Member States shall enjoy such immunities and privileges as are necessary for the independent exercise of their functions.
2. The immunities and privileges under this Article shall be laid down in a separate ASEAN agreement.

Article 19 Immunities and Privileges of the Permanent Representatives and Officials on ASEAN Duties

1. The Permanent Representatives of the Member States to ASEAN and officials of the Member States participating in official ASEAN activities or representing

ASEAN in the Member States shall enjoy such immunities and privileges as are necessary for the exercise of
their functions.

2. The immunities and privileges of the Permanent
   Representatives and officials on ASEAN duties shall be
   governed by the 1961 Vienna Convention on Diplomatic
   Relations or in accordance with the national law of the
   ASEAN Member State concerned.

Chapter VII Decision-Making

Article 20 Consultation and Consensus

1. As a basic principle, decision-making in ASEAN shall be
   based on consultation and consensus.
2. Where consensus cannot be achieved, the ASEAN Summit
   may decide how a specific decision can be made.
3. Nothing in paragraphs 1 and 2 of this Article shall affect the
   modes of decision-making as contained in the relevant
   ASEAN legal instruments.
4. In the case of a serious breach of the Charter or noncompliance, the matter shall be referred to the ASEAN Summit
   for decision.

Article 21 Implementation and Procedure

1. Each ASEAN Community Council shall prescribe its own
   rules of procedure.
2. In the implementation of economic commitments, a formula for flexible participation, including the ASEAN

Minus X formula, may be applied where there is a consensus to do so.

Chapter VIII Settlement of Disputes

Article 22 General Principles

1. Member States shall endeavour to resolve peacefully all disputes in a timely manner through dialogue, consultation and negotiation.
2. ASEAN shall maintain and establish dispute settlement mechanisms in all fields of ASEAN cooperation.

Article 23 Good Offices, Conciliation and Mediation

1. Member States which are parties to a dispute may at any time agree to resort to good offices, conciliation or mediation in order to resolve the dispute within an agreed time limit.
2. Parties to the dispute may request the Chairman of ASEAN or the Secretary-General of ASEAN, acting in an ex-officio capacity, to provide good offices, conciliation or mediation.

Article 24 Dispute Settlement Mechanisms in Specific Instruments

1. Disputes relating to specific ASEAN instruments shall be settled through the mechanisms and procedures provided for in such instruments.

2. Disputes which do not concern the interpretation or application of any ASEAN instrument shall be resolved peacefully in accordance with the Treaty of Amity and Cooperation in Southeast Asia and its rules of procedure.

3. Where not otherwise specifically provided, disputes which concern the interpretation or application of ASEAN economic agreements shall be settled in accordance with the ASEAN Protocol on Enhanced Dispute Settlement Mechanism.

Article 25 Establishment of Dispute Settlement Mechanisms

Where not otherwise specifically provided, appropriate dispute settlement mechanisms, including arbitration, shall be established for disputes which concern the interpretation or application of this Charter and other ASEAN instruments.

Article 26 Unresolved Disputes

When a dispute remains unresolved, after the application of the preceding provisions of this Chapter, this dispute shall be referred to the ASEAN Summit, for its decision.

Article 27 Compliance

1. The Secretary-General of ASEAN, assisted by the ASEAN Secretariat or any other designated ASEAN

body, shall monitor the compliance with the findings, recommendations or decisions resulting from an ASEAN dispute settlement mechanism, and submit a report to the ASEAN Summit.

2. Any Member State affected by non-compliance with the findings, recommendations or decisions resulting from an ASEAN dispute settlement mechanism, may refer the matter to the ASEAN Summit for a decision.

Article 28 United Nations Charter Provisions and Other Relevant International Procedures

Unless otherwise provided for in this Charter, Member States have the right of recourse to the modes of peaceful settlement contained in Article 33(1) of the Charter of the United Nations or any other international legal instruments to which the disputing Member States are parties.

Chapter IX Budget and Finance

Article 29 General Principles

1. ASEAN shall establish financial rules and procedures in accordance with international standards.
2. ASEAN shall observe sound financial management policies and practices and budgetary discipline.
3. Financial accounts shall be subject to internal and external audits.

Article 30 Operational Budget and Finances of the ASEAN Secretariat

1. The ASEAN Secretariat shall be provided with the necessary financial resources to perform its functions effectively.
2. The operational budget of the ASEAN Secretariat shall be met by ASEAN Member States through equal annual contributions which shall be remitted in a timely manner.
3. The Secretary-General shall prepare the annual operational budget of the ASEAN Secretariat for approval by the ASEAN Coordinating Council upon the recommendation of the Committee of Permanent Representatives.
4. The ASEAN Secretariat shall operate in accordance with the financial rules and procedures determined by the ASEAN Coordinating Council upon the recommendation of the Committee of Permanent Representatives.

Chapter X Administration and Procedure

Article 31 Chairman of ASEAN

1. The Chairmanship of ASEAN shall rotate annually, based on the alphabetical order of the English names of Member States.
2. ASEAN shall have, in a calendar year, a single Chairmanship by which the Member State assuming the Chairmanship shall chair:

(a) the ASEAN Summit and related summits;
(b) the ASEAN Coordinating Council;

(c) the three ASEAN Community Councils;

(d) where appropriate, the relevant ASEAN Sectoral Ministerial Bodies and senior officials; and

(e) the Committee of Permanent Representatives.

Article 32 Role of the Chairman of ASEAN

The Member State holding the Chairmanship of ASEAN shall:

(a) actively promote and enhance the interests and wellbeing of ASEAN, including efforts to build an ASEAN Community through policy initiatives, coordination, consensus and cooperation;

(b) ensure the centrality of ASEAN;

(c) ensure an effective and timely response to urgent issues or crisis situations affecting ASEAN, including providing its good offices and such other arrangements to immediately address these concerns;

(d) represent ASEAN in strengthening and promoting closer relations with external partners; and

(e) carry out such other tasks and functions as may be mandated.

Article 33 Diplomatic Protocol and Practices

ASEAN and its Member States shall adhere to existing diplomatic protocol and practices in the conduct of all activities relating to ASEAN. Any changes shall be approved by the ASEAN Coordinating Council upon the recommendation of the Committee of Permanent Representatives.

Article 34 Working Language of ASEAN

The working language of ASEAN shall be English.

Chapter XI Identity and Symbols

Article 35 ASEAN Identity

ASEAN shall promote its common ASEAN identity and a sense of belonging among its peoples in order to achieve its shared destiny, goals and values.

Article 36 ASEAN Motto

The ASEAN motto shall be: 'One Vision, One Identity, One Community'.

Article 37 ASEAN Flag

The ASEAN flag shall be as shown in Annex 3.

Article 38 ASEAN Emblem

The ASEAN emblem shall be as shown in Annex 4.

Article 39 ASEAN Day

The eighth of August shall be observed as ASEAN Day.

Article 40 ASEAN Anthem

ASEAN shall have an anthem.

APPENDICES

Chapter XII External Relations

Article 41 Conduct of External Relations

1. ASEAN shall develop friendly relations and mutually beneficial dialogue, cooperation and partnerships with countries and sub-regional, regional and international
organisations and institutions.
2. The external relations of ASEAN shall adhere to the purposes and principles set forth in this Charter.
3. ASEAN shall be the primary driving force in regional
arrangements that it initiates and maintain its centrality
in regional cooperation and community building.
4. In the conduct of external relations of ASEAN, Member
States shall, on the basis of unity and solidarity, coordinate
and endeavour to develop common positions and pursue
joint actions.
5. The strategic policy directions of ASEAN's external relations shall be set by the ASEAN Summit upon the recommendation of the ASEAN Foreign Ministers Meeting.
6. The ASEAN Foreign Ministers Meeting shall ensure consistency and coherence in the conduct of ASEAN's external
relations.
7. ASEAN may conclude agreements with countries or sub-
regional, regional and international organisations and
institutions. The procedures for concluding such agreements shall be prescribed by the ASEAN Coordinating
Council in consultation with the ASEAN Community
Councils.

Article 42 Dialogue Coordinator

1. Member States, acting as Country Coordinators, shall take turns to take overall responsibility in coordinating and promoting the interests of ASEAN in its relations with the relevant Dialogue Partners, regional and international organisations and institutions.

2. In relations with the external partners, the Country Coordinators shall, inter alia:

   (a) represent ASEAN and enhance relations on the basis of mutual respect and equality, in conformity with ASEAN's principles;

   (b) co-chair relevant meetings between ASEAN and external partners; and

   (c) be supported by the relevant ASEAN Committees in Third Countries and International Organisations.

Article 43 ASEAN Committees in Third Countries and International Organisations

1. ASEAN Committees in Third Countries may be established in non-ASEAN countries comprising heads of diplomatic missions of ASEAN Member States. Similar Committees may be established relating to international organisations. Such Committees shall promote ASEAN's interests and identity in the host countries and international organisations.

2. The ASEAN Foreign Ministers Meeting shall determine the rules of procedure of such Committees.

Article 44 Status of External Parties

1. In conducting ASEAN's external relations, the ASEAN Foreign Ministers Meeting may confer on an external party the formal status of Dialogue Partner, Sectoral Dialogue Partner, Development Partner, Special Observer, Guest, or other status that may be established henceforth.
2. External parties may be invited to ASEAN meetings or cooperative activities without being conferred any formal status, in accordance with the rules of procedure.

Article 45 Relations with the United Nations System and Other International Organisations and Institutions

1. ASEAN may seek an appropriate status with the United Nations system as well as with other sub-regional, regional, international organisations and institutions.
2. The ASEAN Coordinating Council shall decide on the participation of ASEAN in other sub-regional, regional, international organisations and institutions.

Article 46 Accreditation of Non-ASEAN Member States to ASEAN

Non-ASEAN Member States and relevant inter-governmental organisations may appoint and accredit Ambassadors to ASEAN. The ASEAN Foreign Ministers Meeting shall decide on such accreditation.

Chapter XIII General and Final Provisions

Article 47 Signature, Ratification, Depository and Entry Into Force

1. This Charter shall be signed by all ASEAN Member States.
2. This Charter shall be subject to ratification by all ASEAN Member States in accordance with their respective internal procedures.
3. Instruments of ratification shall be deposited with the Secretary-General of ASEAN who shall promptly notify all Member States of each deposit.
4. This Charter shall enter into force on the thirtieth day following the date of deposit of the tenth instrument of ratification with the Secretary-General of ASEAN.

Article 48 Amendments

1. Any Member State may propose amendments to the Charter.
2. Proposed amendments to the Charter shall be submitted by the ASEAN Coordinating Council by consensus to the ASEAN Summit for its decision.
3. Amendments to the Charter agreed to by consensus by the ASEAN Summit shall be ratified by all Member States in accordance with Article 47.
4. An amendment shall enter into force on the thirtieth day following the date of deposit of the last instrument of ratification with the Secretary-General of ASEAN.

Article 49 Terms of Reference and Rules of Procedure

Unless otherwise provided for in this Charter, the ASEAN Coordinating Council shall determine the terms of reference and rules of procedure and shall ensure their consistency.

Article 50 Review

This Charter may be reviewed five years after its entry into force or as otherwise determined by the ASEAN Summit.

Article 51 Interpretation of the Charter

1. Upon the request of any Member State, the interpretation of the Charter shall be undertaken by the ASEAN Secretariat in accordance with the rules of procedure determined by the ASEAN Coordinating Council.
2. Any dispute arising from the interpretation of the Charter shall be settled in accordance with the relevant provisions in Chapter VIII.
3. Headings and titles used throughout the Charter shall only be for the purpose of reference.

Article 52 Legal Continuity

1. All treaties, conventions, agreements, concords, declarations, protocols and other ASEAN instruments which have been in effect before the entry into force of this Charter shall continue to be valid.

2. In case of inconsistency between the rights and obligations of ASEAN Member States under such instruments and this Charter, the Charter shall prevail.

Article 53 Original Text

The signed original text of this Charter in English shall be deposited with the Secretary-General of ASEAN, who shall provide a certified copy to each Member State.

Article 54 Registration of the ASEAN Charter

This Charter shall be registered by the Secretary-General of ASEAN with the Secretariat of the United Nations, pursuant to Article 102, paragraph 1 of the Charter of the United Nations.

Article 55 ASEAN Assets

The assets and funds of the Organisation shall be vested in the name of ASEAN.

DONE in Singapore on the Twentieth Day of November in the Year Two Thousand and Seven, in a single original in the English language.

For Brunei Darussalam: **HAJI HASSANAL BOLKIAH**,
  Sultan of Brunei Darussalam
For the Kingdom of Cambodia: **SAMDECH HUN SEN**,
  Prime Minister
For the Republic of Indonesia: **DR. SUSILO BAMBANG YUDHOYONO**, President

For the Lao People's Democratic Republic: **BOUASONE BOUPHAVANH**, Prime Minister

For Malaysia: **DATO' SERI ABDULLAH AHMAD BADAWI**, Prime Minister

For the Union of Myanmar: **GENERAL THEIN SEIN**, Prime Minister

For the Republic of the Philippines: **GLORIA MACAPAGAL-ARROYO**, President

For the Republic of Singapore: **LEE HSIEN LOONG**, Prime Minister

For the Kingdom of Thailand: **GENERAL SURAYUD CHULANONT (RET.)** Prime Minister

For the Socialist Republic of Viet Nam: **NGUYEN TAN DUNG**, Prime Minister

Annex 1 – ASEAN Sectoral Ministerial Bodies

I ASEAN Political-Security Community

1. ASEAN Foreign Ministers Meeting (AMM)
   - ASEAN Senior Officials Meeting (ASEAN SOM)
   - ASEAN Standing Committee (ASC)
   - Senior Officials Meeting on Development Planning (SOMDP)
2. Commission on the Southeast Asia Nuclear Weapons-Free Zone (SEANWFZ Commission)
   - Executive Committee on the SEANWZ
3. ASEAN Defence Ministers Meeting (ADMM)
   - ASEAN Defence Senior Officials Meeting (ADSOM)

4. ASEAN Law Ministers Meeting (ALAWMM)
   - ASEAN Senior Law Officials Meeting (ASLOM)
5. ASEAN Ministerial Meeting on Transnational Crime (AMMTC)
   - Senior Officials Meeting on Transnational Crime (SOMTC)
   - ASEAN Senior Officials on Drugs Matters (ASOD)
   - Directors-General of Immigration Departments and Heads of Consular Affairs Divisions of Ministries of Foreign Affairs Meeting (DGICM)
6. ASEAN Regional Forum (ARF)
   - ASEAN Regional Forum (ARF) Senior Officials Meeting (ARF SOM)

II ASEAN Economic Community

1. ASEAN Economic Ministers Meeting (AEM)
   - High Level Task Force on ASEAN Economic Integration (HLTF-EI)
   - Senior Economic Officials Meeting (SEOM)
2. ASEAN Free Trade Area (AFTA) Council
3. ASEAN Investment Area (AIA) Council
4. ASEAN Finance Ministers Meeting (AFMM)
   - ASEAN Finance and Central Bank Deputies Meeting (AFDM)
   - ASEAN Directors-General of Customs Meeting (Customs DG)
5. ASEAN Ministers Meeting on Agriculture and Forestry (AMAF)
   - Senior Officials Meeting of the ASEAN Ministers on Agriculture and Forestry (SOM-AMAF)

- ASEAN Senior Officials on Forestry (ASOF)
6. ASEAN Ministers on Energy Meeting (AMEM)
   - Senior Officials Meeting on Energy (SOME)
7. ASEAN Ministerial Meeting on Minerals (AMMin)
   - ASEAN Senior Officials Meeting on Minerals (ASOMM)
8. ASEAN Ministerial Meeting on Science and Technology (AMMST)
   - Committee on Science and Technology (COST)
9. ASEAN Telecommunications and Information Technology Ministers Meeting (TELMIN)
   - Telecommunications and Information Technology Senior Officials Meeting (TELSOM)
   - ASEAN Telecommunication Regulators' Council (ATRC)
10. ASEAN Transport Ministers Meeting (ATM)
    - Senior Transport Officials Meeting (STOM)
11. Meeting of the ASEAN Tourism Ministers (M-ATM)
    - Meeting of the ASEAN National Tourism Organisations (ASEAN NTOs)
12. ASEAN Mekong Basin Development Corporation (AMBDC)
    - ASEAN Mekong Basin Development Corporation Steering Committee (AMBDC SC)
    - High Level Finance Committee (HLFC)
13. ASEAN Centre for Energy
14. ASEAN–Japan Centre in Tokyo

III ASEAN Socio-Cultural Community

1. ASEAN Ministers Responsible for Information (AMRI)
   • Senior Officials Meeting Responsible for Information (SOMRI)
2. ASEAN Ministers Responsible for Culture and Arts (AMCA)
   • Senior Officials Meeting for Culture and Arts (SOMCA)
3. ASEAN Education Ministers Meeting (ASED)
   • Senior Officials Meeting on Education (SOM-ED)
4. ASEAN Ministerial Meeting on Disaster Management (AMMDM)
   • ASEAN Committee on Disaster Management (ACDM)
5. ASEAN Ministerial Meeting on the Environment (AMME)
   • ASEAN Senior Officials on the Environment (ASOEN)
6. Conference of the Parties to the ASEAN Agreement on Transboundary Haze Pollution
   • Committee under the COP to the ASEAN Agreement on Transboundary Haze Pollution
7. ASEAN Health Ministers Meeting
   • Senior Officials Meeting on Health Development (SOMHD)
8. ASEAN Labour Ministers Meeting (ALMM)
   • Senior Labour Officials Meeting (SLOM)
   • ASEAN Committee on the Implementation of the ASEAN Declaration on the Protection and Promotion of the Rights of Migrant Workers
9. ASEAN Ministers on Rural Development and Poverty Eradication (AMRDPE)

- Senior Officials Meeting on Rural Development and Poverty Eradication (SOMRDPE)
10. ASEAN Ministerial Meeting on Social Welfare and Development (AMMSWD)
    - Senior Officials Meeting on Social Welfare and Development (SOMSWD)
11. ASEAN Ministerial Meeting on Youth (AMMY)
    - Senior Officials Meeting on Youth (SOMY)
12. ASEAN Conference on Civil Service Matters (ACCSM)
13. ASEAN Centre for Biodiversity (ACB)
14. ASEAN Coordinating Centre for Humanitarian Assistance on Disaster Management (AHA Centre)
15. ASEAN Earthquakes Information Centre
16. ASEAN Specialised Meteorological Centre (ASCM)
17. ASEAN University Network (AUN)

3 ASEAN Monitoring Mechanisms

Year	Name	Community	Purpose	Section
1976	Declaration of ASEAN Concord	Political-Security	Symbolism	1.2.1.1
1977	Agreement on ASEAN Preferential Trading Arrangements	Economic	Facilitation	1.1.1.1
1980	Basic Agreement on ASEAN Industrial Projects	Economic	Facilitation	1.1.1.2

Year	Name	Community	Purpose	Section
1985	Agreement on the Conservation of Nature and Natural Resources	Socio-Cultural	Symbolism	1.3.2.1
1987	Jakarta Resolution on Sustainable Development	Socio-Cultural	Facilitation	1.3.2.2
1988	Memorandum of Understanding Regarding the ASEAN Grain Post-Harvest Programme	Economic	Facilitation	1.1.1.3
1992	Framework Agreements on Enhancing ASEAN Economic Cooperation	Economic	Interpretation	1.1.1.4
1992	Agreement on the Common Effective Preferential Tariff (CEPT) Scheme for the ASEAN Free Trade Area	Economic	Implementation	1.1.1.5
1995	ASEAN Customs Code of Conduct	Economic	Facilitation	1.1.1.6
1995	ASEAN Framework Agreement on Services	Economic	Interpretation	1.1.1.7
1995	ASEAN Framework Agreement on Intellectual Property Cooperation	Economic	Interpretation	1.1.1.8

Year	Name	Community	Purpose	Section
1995	Southeast Asia Nuclear-Weapon-Free Zone Treaty	Political-Security	Compliance	1.2.2.1
1996	Basic Agreement on the ASEAN Industrial Cooperation Scheme	Economic	Symbolism	1.1.1.9
1998	Framework Agreement on the ASEAN Investment Area	Economic	Interpretation	1.1.1.10
1998	ASEAN Framework Agreement on the Facilitation of Goods in Transit	Economic	Interpretation	1.1.1.11
2002	Framework Agreement on Comprehensive Economic Co-Operation Between ASEAN and the People's Republic of China	Economic	Interpretation	1.1.1.12
2002	ASEAN Memorandum of Understanding on the Trans-ASEAN Gas	Economic	Implementation	1.1.1.13
2003	Declaration of ASEAN Concord II (Bali Concord II)	Political-Security	Symbolism	1.2.1.2

Year	Name	Community	Purpose	Section
2004	Agreement on Trade in Goods of the Framework Agreement on Comprehensive Economic Co-operation between the Association of Southeast Asian Nations and the People's Republic of China	Economic	Implementation	1.1.1.14
2004	ASEAN Framework Agreement for the Integration of Priority Sectors	Economic	Interpretation	1.1.1.15
2004	ASEAN Security Community Plan of Action	Political-Security	Implementation	1.2.1.3
2004	Declaration on the Elimination of Violence Against Women in the ASEAN Region	Political-Security	Symbolism	1.2.4.1
2004	Malacca Strait Patrols	Political-Security	Compliance	1.2.5.1
2005	ASEAN Baseline Report (ABR)	Economic	Facilitation	1.1.2.1
2005	Aceh Monitoring Mission (AMM)	Political-Security	Compliance	1.2.5.2

Year	Name	Community	Purpose	Section
2005	ASEAN Agreement on Disaster Management and Emergency Response	Socio-Cultural	Symbolism	1.3.2.4
2007	Memorandum of Understanding Between the Association of Southeast Asian Nations and the Government of the People's Republic of China on Strengthening Sanitary and Phytosanitary Cooperation	Economic	Symbolism	1.1.1.16
2007	ASEAN Mutual Recognition Arrangement on Architectural Services	Economic	Symbolism	1.1.1.17
2007	Memorandum of Understanding on the ASEAN Power Grid	Economic	Implementation	1.1.1.18
2007	ASEAN Community Progress Monitoring System	Economic	Facilitation	1.1.2.2
2007	ASEAN Convention on Counter Terrorism	Political-Security	Implementation	1.2.3.1

Year	Name	Community	Purpose	Section
2007	ASEAN Declaration on the Protection and Promotion of the Rights of Migrant Workers	Political-Security	Facilitation	1.2.4.2
2007	ASEAN Community Progress Monitoring System	Socio-Cultural	Facilitation	1.3.1.1
2008	Thailand–Cambodia Border Dispute	Political-Security	Symbolism	1.2.5.3
2009	ASEAN Trade in Goods Agreement (ATIGA)	Economic	Compliance	1.1.1.19
2009	ASEAN Comprehensive Investment Agreement (ACIA)	Economic	Compliance	1.1.1.20
2009	Agreement on Trade in Goods Under the Framework Agreement on Comprehensive Economic Cooperation between the Association of Southeast Asian Nations and the Republic of India	Economic	Facilitation	1.1.1.21

Year	Name	Community	Purpose	Section
2009	Agreement on Investment of the Framework Agreement on Comprehensive Economic Cooperation Between the People's Republic of China and the Association of Southeast Asian Nations	Economic	Implementation	1.1.1.22
2009	ASEAN Multilateral Agreement on Air Services	Economic	Facilitation	1.1.1.23
2009	Cha-am Hua Hin Declaration on the Roadmap for the ASEAN Community	Political-Security	Implementation	1.2.1.4
2009	Blueprint on the ASEAN Political-Security Community	Political-Security	Facilitation	1.2.1.5
2009	ASEAN Intergovernmental Commission on Human Rights	Political-Security	Facilitation	1.2.4.3
2009	ASEAN Socio-Cultural Community Blueprint	Socio-Cultural	Facilitation	1.3.1.2

Year	Name	Community	Purpose	Section
2010	AEC Scorecard (in collaboration with ERIA)	Economic	Facilitation	1.1.2.3
2011	ASEAN Integration Monitoring Office (AIMO)	Economic	Facilitation	1.1.2.4
2011	ASEAN+3 Macroeconomic Research Office (AMRO)	Economic	Compliance (& Facilitation)	1.1.2.5
2012	ASEAN Election Observation Mission to Myanmar	Political-Security	Symbolism	1.2.5.4

BIBLIOGRAPHY

Treaties and Agreements

Convention Relative to the Protection of Civilian Persons in Time of War (Fourth Geneva Convention), done at Geneva, 12 August 1949, available at www.icrc.org/ihl.

International Covenant on Civil and Political Rights (ICCPR), 16 December 1966, 999 UNTS 171, in force 23 March 1976, available at www.ohchr.org/EN/ProfessionalInterest/Pages/CCPR.aspx.

The ASEAN Declaration (Bangkok Declaration), Indonesia–Malaysia–Philippines–Singapore–Thailand, done at Bangkok, 8 August 1967, available at http://cil.nus.edu.sg/1967/1967-asean-declaration-signed-on-8-august-1967-by-the-foreign-ministers.

Declaration on the Zone of Peace, Freedom and Neutrality (ZOPFAN), done at Kuala Lumpur, 27 November 1971, available at http://cil.nus.edu.sg/1971/1971-zone-of-peace-freedom-and-neutrality-declaration-signed-on-27-november-1971-in-kuala-lumpur-malaysia-by-the-foreign-ministers.

Agreement on the Establishment of the ASEAN Secretariat, done at Bali, 24 February 1976, available at http://cil.nus.edu.sg/1976/1976-agreement-on-the-establishment-of-the-asean-secretariat-signed-on-24-february-1976-in-bali-indonesia-by-the-foreign-ministers/.

Declaration of ASEAN Concord, done at Bali, 24 February 1976, available at http://cil.nus.edu.sg/1976/1976-declaration-of-asean-concord-signed-on-24-february-1976-in-bali-indonesia-by-the-heads-of-stategovernment/.

Treaty of Amity and Cooperation in Southeast Asia, done at Denpasar, 24 February 1976, available at www.asean.org/news/item/treaty-of-amity-and-cooperation-in-southeast-asia-indonesia-24-february-1976-3.

Agreement on ASEAN Preferential Trading Arrangements, done at Manila, 24 February 1977, available at www.aseansec.org/1376.htm.

Convention on the Elimination of All Forms of Discrimination against Women, 18 December 1979, UN Doc. A/34/46, in force 3 September 1981, available at www1.umn.edu/humanrts/instree/e1cedaw.htm.

Basic Agreement on ASEAN Industrial Projects, done at Kuala Lumpur, 6 March 1980, available at www.aseansec.org/1362.htm.

ASEAN Customs Code of Conduct, done at Jakarta, 18 March 1983, available at www.asean.org/communities/asean-economic-community/item/asean-customs-code-of-conduct-jakarta-18-march-1983-2.

Agreement on the Conservation of Nature and Natural Resources, done at Kuala Lumpur, 9 July 1985, available at http://cil.nus.edu.sg/1985/1985-agreement-on-the-conservation-of-nature-and-natural-resources-signed-on-9-july-1985-in-kuala-lumpur-malaysia-by-the-foreign-ministers.

Jakarta Resolution on Sustainable Development, done at Jakarta, 30 October 1987, available at http://environment.asean.org/jakarta-resolution-on-sustainable-development.

Memorandum of Understanding between the Government of the Kingdom of Thailand, The Association of Southeast Asian Nations (ASEAN) and the Government of Canada Regarding the ASEAN Grain Post-Harvest Programme, done at Bangkok, 8 July 1988, available at www.asean.org/communities/asean-economic-community/item/memorandum-of-understanding-between-the-government-of-the-kingdom-of-thailand-the-association-of-southeast-asian-nations-aseapi-and-the-government-of-canada-regarding-the-asean-grain-post-harvest-programme-bangkok-thailand-8-july-1988.

Protocol Amending the Agreement of the Establishment of the ASEAN Secretariat, done at Bandar Seri Begawan, 4 July 1989, available at www.asean.org/news/item/asean-secretariat-basic-documents-protocol-amending-the-agreement-of-the-establish ment-of-the-asean-secretariat-bandar-seri-begawan-brunei-dar ussalam-4-july-1989-2.

Agreement on the Common Effective Preferential Tariff (CEPT) Scheme for the ASEAN Free Trade Area, done at Singapore, 28 January 1992, available at www.aseansec.org/1164.htm.

Framework Agreements on Enhancing ASEAN Economic Cooperation, done at Singapore, 28 January 1992, available at www.aseansec.org/12374.htm.

Protocol Amending the Agreement on the Establishment of the ASEAN Secretariat, done at Manila, 22 July 1992, available at http://cil.nus.edu.sg/1992/1992-protocol-amending-the-agree ment-on-the-establishment-of-the-asean-secretariat-signed-on-22-july-1992-in-manila-the-philippines-by-the-foreign-ministers/.

Rio Declaration on Environment and Development, 12 August 1992, UN Doc. A/CONF.151/26 (Vol. I), Annex I, available at www.un.org/documents/ga/confi51/aconf15126-1annex1.htm.

ASEAN Customs Code of Conduct, done at Tretes, Indonesia, 18 July 1995, available at www.aseansec.org/2165.htm.

ASEAN Framework Agreement on Intellectual Property Cooperation, done at Bangkok, 15 December 1995, available at http://cil.nus.edu.sg/1995/1995-asean-framework-agreement-on-intellectual-property-cooperation-signed-on-15-december-1995-in-bangkok-thailand-by-the-economic-ministers.

ASEAN Framework Agreement on Services, done at Bangkok, 15 December 1995, available at www.asean.org/communities/asean-economic-community/item/asean-framework-agreement-on-services.

Southeast Asia Nuclear-Weapon-Free Zone Treaty (Bangkok Treaty/SEANWFZ), done at Bangkok, 15 December 1995, in force 28 March 1997, available at http://cil.nus.edu.sg/1995/1995-treaty-on-the-southeast-asia-nuclear-weapon-free-zone-signed-on-15-december-1995-in-bangkok-thailand-by-the-heads-of-stategovernment.

ASEAN Protocol on Dispute Settlement Mechanism, done at Manila, 20 November 1996, in force 26 May 1998, available at www.aseansec.org/16654.htm.

Basic Agreement on the ASEAN Industrial Cooperation Scheme, done at Singapore, 27 April 1996, available at http://cil.nus.edu.sg/1996/1996-basic-agreement-on-the-asean-industrial-cooperation-scheme-signed-on-27-april-1996-in-singapore-by-the-economic-ministers.

ASEAN Declaration on Transnational Crime, done at Manila, 20 December 1997, available at http://cil.nus.edu.sg/1997/1997-asean-declaration-on-transnational-crime-signed-on-20-december-1997-in-manila-philippines.

Regional Haze Action Plan, done at Singapore, 23 December 1997, available at http://cil.nus.edu.sg/rp/pdf/1997%20Regional%20Haze%20Action%20Plan-pdf.pdf.

ASEAN Framework Agreement on the Facilitation of Goods in Transit, done at Hanoi, 16 December 1998, available at www.aseansec.org/7377.htm.

Framework Agreement on the ASEAN Investment Area, done at Makati, Philippines, 7 October 1998, available at www.aseansec.org/7994.pdf.

ASEAN Declaration on Joint Action to Counter Terrorism, done at Bandar Seri Begawan, Brunei Darussalam, 5 November 2001, available at http://cil.nus.edu.sg/2001/2001-asean-declaration-on-joint-action-to-counter-terrorism-signed-on-5-november-2001-in-bandar-seri-begawan-brunei-darussalam.

ASEAN Agreement on Transboundary Haze Pollution, done at Kuala Lumpur, 10 June 2002, in force 11 November 2003, available at http://haze.asean.org/hazeagreement.

The ASEAN Memorandum of Understanding (MOU) on the Trans-ASEAN Gas, done at Bali, 5 July 2002, available at www.asean.org/communities/asean-economic-community/item/the-asean-memorandum-of-understanding-mou-on-the-trans-asean-gas.

Framework Agreement on Comprehensive Economic Co-Operation Between ASEAN and the People's Republic of China, done at Phnom Penh, 4 November 2002, available at www.asean.org/communities/asean-economic-community/item/framework-agreement-on-comprehensive-economic-co-operation-between-asean-and-the-people-s-republic-of-china-phnom-penh-4-november-2002-3.

(ASEAN–EU) Joint Declaration on Cooperation to Combat Terrorism, done at Brussels, 28 January 2003, available at http://cil.nus.edu.sg/2003/2003-joint-declaration-on-cooperation-to-combat-terrorism.

ASEAN–India Joint Declaration for Cooperation to Combat International Terrorism, done at Bali, 8 October 2003, available at http://cil.nus.edu.sg/2003/2003-asean-india-joint-declaration-for-cooperation-to-combat-international-terrorism.

Declaration of ASEAN Concord II, done at Bali, 7 October 2003, available at www.asean.org/news/item/declaration-of-asean-concord-ii-bali-concord-ii.

Agreement on Trade in Goods of the Framework Agreement on Comprehensive Economic Co-operation between the

Association of Southeast Asian Nations and the People's Republic of China, done at Vientiane, 29 November 2004, available at www.aseansec.org/16646.htm.

ASEAN–Australia Joint Declaration for Cooperation to Combat International Terrorism, done at Jakarta, 2 July 2004, available at http://cil.nus.edu.sg/2004/2004-asean-australia-joint-declaration-for-cooperation-to-combat-international-terrorism.

ASEAN Framework Agreement for the Integration of Priority Sectors, done at Vientiane, 29 November 2004, available at http://cil.nus.edu.sg/2004/2004-asean-framework-agreement-for-the-integration-of-priority-sectors-signed-on-29-november-2004-in-vientiane-laos-by-the-heads-of-stategovernment.

ASEAN Protocol on Enhanced Dispute Settlement Mechanism, done at Vientiane, 29 November 2004, in force 29 November 2004, available at www.aseansec.org/16754.htm.

ASEAN Security Community Plan of Action, done at Vientiane, 29 November 2004, available at www.asean.org/news/item/asean-security-community-plan-of-action.

Declaration on the Elimination of Violence Against Women in the ASEAN Region done at Jakarta, 30 June 2004, available at www.asean.org/news/item/declaration-on-the-elimination-of-violence-against-women-in-the-asean-region-2.

Resolution Conf. 11.17 (Rev. CoP16), 'National Reports' (Convention on International Trade in Endangered Species of Wild Fauna and Flora (CITES), 2004), available at www.cites.org/eng/res/11/11-17R16.php.

Vientiane Action Programme 2004–2010, done at Vientiane, 29 November 2004, available at http://cil.nus.edu.sg/2004/2004-vientiane-action-programme-2004-2010-signed-on-29-november-2004-in-vientiane-laos-by-the-heads-of-stategovernment-vap.

155

ASEAN Agreement on Disaster Management and Emergency Response, done at Vientiane, 26 July 2005, available at http://cil.nus.edu.sg/2005/2005-asean-agreement-on-disaster-manage ment-and-emergency-response-signed-on-26-july-2005-in-vien tiane-laos-by-the-foreign-ministers-2.

ASEAN Baseline Report: Measurements to Monitor Progress Towards the ASEAN Community (Jakarta: ASEAN Secretariat, November 2005), available at www.aseansec.org/ABR.pdf.

ASEAN–New Zealand Joint Declaration for Cooperation to Combat International Terrorism, done at Vientiane, 29 July 2005, available at http://cil.nus.edu.sg/2005/2005-asean-new-zealand-joint-declaration-for-cooperation-to-combat-interna tional-terrorism.

ASEAN–Republic of Korea Joint Declaration for Cooperation to Combat International Terrorism, done at Vientiane, 2005, avail-able at http://cil.nus.edu.sg/2005/2005-asean%e2%80%93repub lic-of-korea-joint-declaration-for-cooperation-to-combat-inter national-terrorism.

Council Joint Action 2005/643/CFSP of 9 September 2005 on the European Union Monitoring Mission in Aceh (Indonesia) (Aceh Monitoring Mission – AMM), done at Brussels, 9 September 2005, available at www.aceh-mm.org/download/ english/Council%20Joint%20Action.pdf.

Memorandum of Understanding Between the Government of Indonesia and the Free Aceh Movement, done at Helsinki, 15 August 2005, available at www.aceh-mm.org/download/ english/Helsinki%20MoU.pdf.

ASEAN–Canada Joint Declaration for Cooperation to Combat International Terrorism, done at Kuala Lumpur, 28 July 2006, available at http://cil.nus.edu.sg/2006/2006-asean-canada-joint-declaration-for-cooperation-to-combat-international-terrorism.

Report of the Eminent Persons Group on the ASEAN Charter (Jakarta: ASEAN, December 2006), available at www.asean sec.org/19247.pdf.

ASEAN Convention on Counter Terrorism, done at Cebu, Philippines, 13 January 2007, available at http://cil.nus.edu.sg/2007/2007-asean-convention-on-counter-terrorism-signed-on-13-january-2007-in-cebu-philippines-by-the-heads-of-stategovernment.

ASEAN Declaration on the Protection and Promotion of the Rights of Migrant Workers, done at Cebu, Philippines, 13 January 2007, available at http://cil.nus.edu.sg/2007/2007-asean-declaration-on-the-protection-and-promotion-of-the-rights-of-migrant-workers-signed-on-13-january-2007-in-cebu-philippines-by-the-heads-of-stategovernment.

ASEAN Defence Ministers' Meeting Three-Year Work Programme, done at Singapore, 14 November 2007, available at http://cil.nus.edu.sg/2007/2007-asean-defence-ministers%e2%80%99-meeting-three-year-work-programme-adopted-on-14-november-2007-in-singapore-by-the-defence-ministers.

ASEAN Mutual Recognition Arrangement on Architectural Services, done at Singapore, 19 November 2007, available at www.aseansec.org/21137.pdf.

Charter of the Association of Southeast Asian Nations (ASEAN Charter), done at Singapore, 20 November 2007, in force 15 December 2008, available at www.asean.org/archive/publica tions/ASEAN-Charter.pdf.

East Asian Strategic Review (Tokyo: National Institute for Defence Studies, 2007), available at www.nids.go.jp/english/publica tion/east-asian/e2007.html.

Memorandum of Understanding Between the Association of Southeast Asian Nations and the Government of the People's Republic of China on Strengthening Sanitary and Phytosanitary

Cooperation, done at Singapore, 20 November 2007, available at www.asean.org/archive/21089.pdf.

Memorandum of Understanding on the ASEAN Power Grid, done at Singapore, 23 August 2007, available at www.asean.org/communities/asean-economic-community/item/memoran dum-of-understanding-on-the-asean-power-grid.

ASEAN Community Progress Monitoring System: Country Indicators (Jakarta: ASEAN Secretariat, June 2008), available at www.asean.org/archive/publications/ACPMS-2.pdf.

ASEAN Community Progress Monitoring System: Pan-ASEAN Indicators (Jakarta: ASEAN Secretariat, June 2008), available at www.asean.org/archive/publications/ACPMS-1.pdf.

Letter dated 22 July 2008 from the Permanent Representative of Thailand to the United Nations addressed to the President of the Security Council, UN Doc. S/2008/478 (2008).

Agreement on Investment of the Framework Agreement on Comprehensive Economic Cooperation Between the People's Republic of China and the Association of Southeast Asian Nations, done at Bangkok, 15 August 2009, available at www.aseansec.org/22974.pdf.

Agreement on Trade in Goods Under the Framework Agreement on Comprehensive Economic Cooperation between the Association of Southeast Asian Nations and the Republic of India, done at Bangkok, 13 August 2009, available at www.aseansec.org/22677.pdf.

ASEAN Comprehensive Investment Agreement (ACIA), done at Cha-am, Thailand, 26 February 2009, available at http://cil.nus.edu.sg/2009/2009-asean-comprehensive-investment-agree ment-signed-on-26-february-2009-in-cha-am-thailand-by-the-economic-ministers/.

ASEAN Framework Agreement on the Facilitation of Inter-State Transport, done at Manila, 10 December 2009, available at http://cil.nus.edu.sg/rp/pdf/2009%20ASEAN%20Framework %20Agreement%20on%20the%20Facilitation%20of%20Inter-State%20Transport-pdf.pdf.

ASEAN Intergovernmental Commission on Human Rights (Terms of Reference) (Jakarta: ASEAN, October 2009), available at www.asean.org/images/archive/publications/TOR-of-AICHR.pdf.

ASEAN Multilateral Agreement on Air Services, done at Manila, 20 May 2009, available at www.asean.org/communities/asean-economic-community/item/asean-multilateral-agreement-on-air-services-manila-20-may-2009-2.

ASEAN Multilateral Agreement on the Full Liberalisation of Air Freight Services, done at Manila, 20 May 2009, available at www.asean.org/communities/asean-economic-community/item/asean-multilateral-agreement-on-the-full-liberalisation-of-air-freight-services-manila-20-may-2009.

ASEAN Political-Security Community Blueprint (Jakarta: ASEAN, June 2009), available at www.asean.org/archive/5187-18.pdf.

ASEAN Socio-Cultural Community Blueprint (Jakarta: ASEAN, June 2009), available at www.asean.org/archive/5187-19.pdf.

ASEAN Trade in Goods Agreement (ATIGA), done at Cha-am, Thailand, 26 February 2009, available at www.asean.org/communities/asean-economic-community/category/asean-trade-in-goods-agreement.

Cha-am Hua Hin Declaration on the Roadmap for the ASEAN Community, done at Cha-am, Thailand, 1 March 2009, available at www.asean.org/news/item/cha-am-hua-hin-declaration-on-the-roadmap-for-the-asean-community-2009-2015.

Declaration on the Intergovernmental Commission on Human Rights, done at Cha-am Hua Hin, Thailand, 23 October 2009, available at www.asean.org/images/archive/documents/Declaration-AICHR.pdf.

AICHR Five-Year Work Plan 2010–2015 (Jakarta: AICHR, 2010), available at http://aichr.org/documents.

ASEAN Economic Community Scorecard: Charting Progress Towards Regional Economic Integration (Jakarta: ASEAN Secretariat, March 2010), available at www.asean.org/publica tions/AEC%20Scorecard.pdf.

ASEAN Multilateral Agreement on the Full Liberalisation of Passenger Air Services, done at Bander Seri Begawan, Brunei Darussalam, 12 November 2010, available at www.asean.org/ archive/transport/Agreement-101112.pdf.

ASEAN in the Global Community: Annual Report 2010–2011 (Jakarta: ASEAN Secretariat, July 2011), available at www.asean sec.org/publications/AR1011.pdf.

ASEAN Statement at the APEC Ministers Responsible for Trade Meeting (Montana: 20 May 2011), available at www.aseansec. org/26318.htm.

The Joint Ministerial Statement of the 14th ASEAN+3 Finance Ministers' Meeting (Ha Noi, Viet Nam: 4 May 2011), available at www.amro-asia.org/wp-content/uploads/2011/ 11/AFMM3_Hanoi20110504.pdf.

Request for Interpretation of the Judgment of 15 June 1962 in the Case Concerning the Temple of Preah Vihear (Cambodia v. Thailand) (Request for the Indication of Provisional Measures) (18 July 2011), available at www.icj-cij.org.

Security Council Press Statement on Cambodia–Thailand Border Situation, UN Doc. SC/10174 (2011).

Supporting and Enhancing Regional Surveillance for ASEAN+3 and the Chiang Mai Initiative Multilateralization (Manila: Asian Development Bank (ADB), May 2011), available at www.adb.org/sites/default/files/projdocs/2011/42065-02- reg-tar.pdf.

Update Report No. 1: Thailand/Cambodia (New York: Security Council Report, 9 February 2011), available at www.security councilreport.org/update-report/lookup-c-glKWLeMTIsG-b-6552935.php.

ASEAN Economic Community Scorecard: Charting Progress Towards Regional Economic Integration (Jakarta: ASEAN Secretariat, March 2012), available at www.aseansec.org/docu ments/scorecard_final.pdf.

ASEAN Human Rights Declaration, done at Phnom Penh, 18 November 2012, available at www.asean.org/news/asean-state ment-communiques/item/asean-human-rights-declaration.

Books and Articles

Abbott, Frederick M., 'Integration without Institutions: The NAFTA Mutation of the EC Model and the Future of the GATT Regime', *American Journal of Comparative Law*, 40(4) (1992), 917.

Aggarwal, Vinod K. and Jonathan T. Chow, 'The Perils of Consensus: How ASEAN's Meta-Regime Undermines Economic and Environmental Cooperation', *Review of International Political Economy*, 17(2) (2010), 262.

Alter, Karen J. and Laurence R. Helfer, 'The Andean Tribunal of Justice and its Interlocutors: Understanding Preliminary Reference Patterns in the Andean Community', *New York University Journal of International Law and Politics*, 41 (2009), 871.

Arase, David, 'Non-Traditional Security in China–ASEAN Cooperation: The Institutionalization of Regional Security Cooperation and the Evolution of East Asian Regionalism', *Asian Survey*, 50(4) (2010), 808.

Aspinall, Edward, 'Combatants to Contractors: The Political Economy of Peace in Aceh', *Indonesia*, 87 (2009), 1.

Beckman, Robert J. and J. Ashley Roach (eds.), *Piracy and International Maritime Crimes in ASEAN: Prospects for Cooperation* (Cheltenham: Edward Elgar Publishing, 2012).

Beyerlin, Ulrich (ed.), *Ensuring Compliance with Multilateral Environmental Agreements: A Dialogue between Practitioners and Academia* (Leiden: Nijhoff, 2006).

Bradford, John F., 'Shifting the Tides against Piracy in Southeast Asian Waters', *Asian Survey*, 48(3) (2008), 473.

Brown Weiss, Edith (ed.), *International Compliance with Nonbinding Accords* (Washington DC: American Society of International Law, 1997).

Burnett, Erin and James Mahon, 'Monitoring Compliance with International Labor Standards', *Challenge*, 44(2) (2001), 51.

Caballero-Anthony, Mely, 'The ASEAN Charter: An Opportunity Missed or One that Cannot Be Missed?', *Southeast Asian Affairs*, (2008), 71.

Carlsnaes, Walter, Walter Risse and Beth A. Simmons (eds.), *Handbook of International Relations* (London: Sage, 2002).

Chang, Li Lin and Ramkishen S. Rajan, 'The Economics and Politics of Monetary Regionalism in Asia', *ASEAN Economic Bulletin*, 18(1) (2001), 103.

Chesterman, Simon, 'Globalization Rules: Accountability, Power, and the Prospects for Global Administrative Law', *Global Governance*, 14 (2008), 39.

   'The Turn to Ethics: Disinvestment from Multinational Corporations for Human Rights Violations – The Case of Norway's Sovereign Wealth Fund', *American University International Law Review*, 23 (2008), 577.

   'Lawyers, Guns, and Money: The Governance of Business Activities in Conflict Zones', *Chicago Journal of International Law*, 11 (2011), 321.

One Nation under Surveillance: A New Social Contract to Defend Freedom without Sacrificing Liberty (Oxford University Press, 2011).

'The International Court of Justice in Asia: Interpreting the *Temple of Preah Vihear* Case', *Asian Journal of International Law* (2014), available at http://journals.cambridge.org/ article_S204425131400006X.

Choi, JongKu, 'Congratulatory Remarks by Deputy Minister JongKu Choi, Ministry of Strategy and Finance, Republic of Korea' (AMRO, Singapore, 31 January 2012), available at www. amro-asia.org/wp-content/uploads/2012/01/04-Speech-by-Mr-Choi-JongKu.pdf.

Collins, Alan, 'A People-Oriented ASEAN: A Door Ajar or Closed for Civil Society Organizations?', *Contemporary Southeast Asia*, 30(2) (2008), 313.

Davidson, Paul, *ASEAN: The Evolving Legal Framework for Economic Cooperation* (Singapore: Times Academic Press, 2002).

'The ASEAN Way and Role of Law in ASEAN Economic Cooperation', *Singapore Year Book of International Law*, 8 (2004), 165.

Engstrom, David Freeman, 'Harnessing the Private Attorney General: Evidence from Qui Tam Litigation', *Columbia Law Review*, 112 (2012), 1244.

Epstein, Edwin M., 'The Good Company: Rhetoric or Reality? Corporate Social Responsibility and Business Ethics Redux', *American Business Law Journal*, 44 (2007), 207.

Gardner, James, *Legal Imperialism: American Lawyers and Foreign Aid in Latin America* (Madison: University of Wisconsin Press, 1980).

George, Cherian, *Freedom from the Press: Journalism and State Power in Singapore* (Singapore: NUS Press, 2012).

Gil, Ranjit, *ASEAN Towards the 21st Century: A Thirty-Year Review of the Association of Southeast Asian Nations* (London: ASEAN Academic Press, 1997).

Grimes, William, 'The Asian Monetary Fund Reborn? Implications of Chang Mai Initiative Multilateralization', *Asia Policy*, 11 (2011), 79.

Hafez, Zakirul, *The Dimensions of Regional Trade Integration in Southeast Asia* (Ardsley, NY: Transnational Publishers, 2004).

Helfer, Laurence R., 'The Law and Politics of International Delegation: Monitoring Compliance with Unratified Treaties – The ILO Experience', *Law and Contemporary Problems*, 71 (2008), 193.

Hill, Hal and Jayant Menon, 'Financial Safety Nets in Asia: Genesis, Evolution, Adequacy, and Way Forward' (Canberra: Arndt-Corden Department of Economics Crawford School of Public Policy, ANU College of Asia and the Pacific, Working Paper No. 2012/17, September 2012), available at http://crawford.anu.edu.au/acde/publications/publish/papers/wp2012/wp_econ_2012_17.pdf.

Kingsbury, Benedict, Nico Krisch and Richard B. Stewart, 'The Emergence of Global Administrative Law', *Law and Contemporary Problems*, 68 (2005), 15.

Koh Kheng-Lian, 'ASEAN Environmental Protection in Natural Resources and Sustainable Development: Convergence Versus Divergence?', *Macquarie Journal of International and Comparative Environmental Law*, 4 (2007), 43.

Koh Kheng-Lian and Nicholas Robinson, 'Strengthening Sustainable Development in Regional Inter-Governmental Governance: Lessons from the ASEAN Way', *Singapore Journal of International & Comparative Law*, 6 (2002), 640.

Koh, Tommy, 'Is ASEAN Good for the Business Community' (Singapore Chinese Chamber of Commerce & Industry,

Singapore, 14 April 2008), available at http://lkyspp.nus.edu. sg/wp-content/uploads/2013/04/sp_tommykoh_SCCCI-3rd-Distinguished-Speakers-Lecture_14-Apr-08.pdf.

Kooi, Joel Vander, 'The ASEAN Enhanced Dispute Settlement Mechanism', *New York International Law Review*, 20 (2007), 1.

Kwan, Yum K. and Larry D. Qiu, 'The ASEAN+3 Trading Bloc', *Journal of Economic Integration*, 25(1) (2010), 1.

Laffont, Jean-Jacques and Jean Tirole, 'The Politics of Government Decision-Making: A Theory of Regulatory Capture', *Quarterly Journal of Economics*, 106 (1991), 1089.

Lee, Yoong Yoong (ed.), *ASEAN Matters! Reflecting on the Association of Southeast Asian Nations* (Singapore: World Scientific, 2011).

Lombaerde, Philippe de, Antoni Estevadeordal and Kati Suominen (eds.), *Governing Regional Integration for Development: Monitoring Experiences, Methods and Prospects* (Aldershot: Ashgate, 2008).

Mackay, Keith, *How to Build M&E Systems to Support Better Government* (Washington DC: World Bank Independent Evaluation Group, 2007), available at www.worldbank.org/ ieg/ecd/docs/How_to_build_ME_gov.pdf.

Mahbubani, Kishore and Simon Chesterman, 'Asia's Role in Global Governance' (Singapore: World Economic Forum, January 2010), available at http://ssrn.com/abstract=1541364.

Manupipatpong, Worapot, 'The ASEAN Surveillance Process and the East Asian Monetary Fund', *ASEAN Economic Bulletin*, 19(1) (2002), 111.

Manzano, George, 'Is there Any Value-Added in the ASEAN Surveillance Process?', *ASEAN Economic Bulletin*, 18(1) (2001), 94.

McClymont, Mary and Stephen Golub (eds.), *Many Roads to Justice: The Law-Related Work of Ford Foundation Grantees around the World* (New York: Ford Foundation, 2000).

McCubbins, Mathew D. and Thomas Schwartz, 'Congressional Oversight Overlooked: Police Patrols versus Fire Alarms', *American Journal of Political Science*, 28 (1984), 165.

Menon, Ravi, 'Regional Safety Nets to Complement Global Safety Nets' (AMRO, Singapore, 31 January 2012), available at www.amro-asia.org/wp-content/uploads/2012/01/02-Speech-by-Mr-Ravi-Menon.pdf.

Merryman, John H., 'Comparative Law and Social Change: On the Origins, Style, Decline & Revival of the Law and Development Movement', *American Journal of Comparative Law*, 25 (1977), 457.

Mietzner, Marcus, 'Local Elections and Autonomy in Papua and Aceh: Mitigating or Fueling Secessionism?', *Indonesia*, 84 (2007), 1.

Miller, Graham and Louise Twining-Ward, *Monitoring for a Sustainable Tourism Transition: The Challenge of Developing and Using Indicators* (Wallingford: CABI, 2005).

Milne, Rob, 'Multi-Party Monitoring in Ontario: Challenges and Emerging Solutions', *Environments*, 34(1) (2006), 11.

Nair, Deepak, 'ASEAN's Core Norms in the Context of the Global Financial Crisis', *Asian Survey*, 51(2) (2011), 245.

Narine, Shaun, *Explaining ASEAN: Regionalism in Southeast Asia* (Boulder, CO: Lynne Rienner, 2002).

Noortmann, Math, *Enforcing International Law: From Self-Help to Self-Contained Regimes* (Aldershot: Ashgate, 2005).

Pagani, Fabrizio, *Peer Review: A Tool for Co-operation and Change – An Analysis of an OECD Working Method* (Paris: OECD, SG/LEG(2002)1, 11 September 2002), available at www.oecd.org/investment/anti-bribery/anti-briberyconvention/1955285.pdf.

Rajasingham-Senanayake, Darini, 'Transnational Peace Building and Conflict: Lessons from Aceh, Indonesia, and Sri Lanka', *Sojourn: Journal of Social Issues in Southeast Asia*, 24(2) (2009), 211.

Ravenhill, John, 'Economic Cooperation in Southeast Asia: Changing Incentives', *Asian Survey*, 35(9) (1995), 850.

Santoro, Michael A., 'Beyond Codes of Conduct and Monitoring: An Organizational Integrity Approach to Global Labor Practices', *Human Rights Quarterly*, 5(2) (2003), 407.

Satterthwaite, Margaret, 'Human Rights Monitoring, Elections Monitoring, and Electoral Assistance as Preventive Measures', *New York University Journal of International Law and Politics*, 30 (1998), 709.

Seah, Daniel, 'The ASEAN Charter', *International and Comparative Law Quarterly*, 58(1) (2009), 197.

Sen, Rahul and Sadhana Srivastava, 'ASEAN's Bilateral Preferential Trade and Economic Cooperation Agreements: Implications for Asian Economic Integration', *ASEAN Economic Bulletin*, 26(2) (2009), 194.

Severino, Rodolfo, 'Asia Policy Lecture: What ASEAN Is and What It Stands For' (The Research Institute for Asia and the Pacific, University of Sydney, Australia, 22 October 1998), available at www.aseansec.org/3399.htm.

Southeast Asia in Search of an ASEAN Community: Insights from the Former ASEAN Secretary-General (Singapore: ISEAS Publications, 2006).

Simon, Sheldon, 'ASEAN and Multilateralism: The Long, Bumpy Road to Community', *Contemporary Southeast Asia*, 30(2) (2008), 264.

Sornarajah, Muthucumaraswamy and Wang Jiangyu (eds.), *China, India and the International Economic Order* (Cambridge University Press, 2010).

Steiner, Julie E., 'Should "Substitute" Private Attorneys General Enforce Public Environmental Actions? Balancing the Costs and Benefits of the Contingency Fee Environmental Special Counsel Arrangement', *Santa Clara Law Review*, 51 (2011), 853.

Storey, Ian, 'Maritime Security in Southeast Asia: Two Cheers for Regional Cooperation', *Southeast Asian Affairs* (2009), 39.

Stoyanova, Vessela V., 'The Council of Europe's Monitoring Mechanisms and their Relation to Eastern European Member States' Noncompliance', *Santa Clara Law Review*, 45 (2005), 739.

Szasz, Paul C. (ed.), *Administrative and Expert Monitoring of International Treaties* (Ardsley, NY: Transnational Publishers, 1999).

Tamanaha, Brian Z., 'The Lessons of Law-and-Development Studies', *American Journal of International Law*, 89 (1995), 470.

Tan Alan Khee-Jin, 'The ASEAN Agreement on Transboundary Haze Pollution: Prospects for Compliance and Effectiveness in Post-Suharto Indonesia', *New York University Environmental Law Journal*, 13(3) (2005), 647.

Tan Hsien-Li, *The ASEAN Intergovernmental Commission on Human Rights* (Cambridge University Press, 2011).

Tan Lay Hong, 'Will ASEAN Economic Integration Progress Beyond a Free Trade Area?', *International and Comparative Law Quarterly*, 53(4) (2004), 935.

Tan See Seng and Alvin Chew, 'Governing Singapore's Security Sector: Problems, Prospects and Paradox', *Contemporary Southeast Asia*, 30(2) (2008), 241.

Thio Li-ann, 'Implementing Human Rights in ASEAN Countries: Promises to Keep and Miles to Go Before I Sleep', *Yale Human Rights & Development Law Journal*, 2 (1999), 1.

Thorburn, Craig, 'Building Blocks and Stumbling Blocks: Peacebuilding in Aceh, 2005–2009', *Indonesia*, 93 (2012), 83.

Treves, Tullio (ed.), *Civil Society, International Courts and Compliance Bodies* (The Hague: TMC Asser, 2005).

Treves, Tullio, Laura Pineschi, Attila Tanzi, Cesare Pitea, Chiara Ragni and Francesca Romanin Jacur (eds.), *Non-Compliance Procedures and Mechanisms and the Effectiveness of*

International Environmental Agreements (The Hague: T.M.C. Asser Press, 2009).

Trubek, David M. and Marc Galanter, 'Scholars in Self-Estrangement: Some Reflections on the Crisis in Law and Development', *Wisconsin Law Review*, 4 (1974), 1062.

Ulfstein, Geir (ed.), *Making Treaties Work: Human Rights, Environment and Arms Control* (Cambridge University Press, 2007).

Wei Benhua, 'Speech by Mr Wei Benhua, AMRO Director' (AMRO, Singapore, 31 January 2012), available at www.amro-asia.org/wp-content/uploads/2012/01/05-Speech-by-Mr-Wei-Benhua.pdf.

Weissbrodt, David, 'Business and Human Rights', *University of Cincinnati Law Review*, 74 (2005), 55.

Widodo, Tri, 'Market Dynamics in the EU, NAFTA, North East Asia and ASEAN: The Method of Constant Market Shares (CMS) Analysis', *Journal of Economic Integration*, 25(3) (2010), 480.

Wu Shicun, and Zou Keyuan, *Maritime Security in the South China Sea: Regional Implications and International Cooperation* (Aldershot: Ashgate, 2009).

INDEX

arms limitations negotiations, peer monitoring and, 85–6

ASEAN+3 Macroeconomic Research Office (AMRO), 31–3, 63–4, 71–4, 83–4, 86–7

ASEAN Baseline Report (ABR) (2005), 27–8

ASEAN Business Forum (ABF), 70, 88–9

ASEAN Charter (2007), 7–12, 36–7, 108–42

ASEAN–China Trade Negotiation Committee, 19

ASEAN Committee on Trade and Tourism, 12–13

'ASEAN Community', proposal for, 2–3

ASEAN Community Progress Monitoring System (ACPMS) (2007), 28–9, 54, 73–4

ASEAN Comprehensive Investment Agreement (ACIA), 25, 63

ASEAN Consultative Committee for Standards and Quality (ACCSQ), 23–4

ASEAN Convention on Counter Terrorism (2007), 41–3, 65–7, 84–5

ASEAN Co-ordinating Centre for Transboundary Haze Pollution Control, 56–7

ASEAN Coordinating Committee on Investment (CCI), 25

ASEAN Council on Petroleum (ASCOPE), 20

ASEAN Crops Post-Harvest Programme, 13–14, 73–4, 92–3

ASEAN Customs Code of Conduct, 16, 73–4

ASEAN Declaration (1967), 103–7

ASEAN Declaration on the Protection and Promotion of the Rights of Migrant Workers, 44–5, 73–4

ASEAN Declaration on Transnational Crime, 41–3

ASEAN Defence Ministers' Meeting (ADMM), 47–8

ASEAN Economic Community (AEC), 28–9
  Blueprint, 29–30
  compliance *sensu stricto* and, 60–4
  independent regional mechanisms and, 83–4
  Scorecard, 29–30

ASEAN Election Observation Mission to Myanmar, 52

ASEAN Framework Agreement for the Integration of Priority Sectors (2004), 21–2

ASEAN Framework Agreement on Intellectual Property Cooperation, 17

ASEAN Framework Agreement on Services, 16–17
  ASEAN Mutual Recognition Arrangement on Architectural Services, 22

ASEAN Framework Agreement on the Facilitation of Goods in Transit (1998), 19

9 781107 490512